MW01032474

ON THE BLOODSTAINED FIELD

130 Human Interest Stories of the Campaign and Battle of Gettysburg

By Gregory A. Coco

Sketches by John S. Heiser

TABLE OF CONTENTS

FOREWORD

Military historians have a tendency to simplify the past. So it is with the Battle of Gettysburg which has become, for most of us, nothing more than a series of leaders and movements on a map. We are left with faceless soldiers in armies of blue and grey, deified generals distorted in glorifying memoirs and monuments. Compressed and robbed of subtlety, those who fought in America's Civil War are seen illustrating only the most basic emotions — fear, triumph, hope — and nothing so fragile as fatigue, boredom, wonder, or compassion. Ultimately, because the experience of Gettysburg seems ungraspable, it has come to have limited meaning for us.

Until now.

On the pages of On The Bloodstained Field, we are given access to the past identified in human terms. These are new stories for most people; and never before have they been included in one volume. Equal attention is given to men of both armies, to each day of battle and to the lingering aftermath. No story is longer than a paragraph or two, but each is immensely readable and allows the reader to experience the battle through the eyes of men and, in some cases, women who fought at Gettysburg.

Editor Gregory Coco began gathering the stories of Gettysburg as a battlefield guide and later as a ranger/historian for the National Park Service at Gettysburg National Military Park. He continued his research over the years, reading personal accounts, newspapers of the time, and numerous reminiscences of veterans written at their reunions. Surely few men know as much about the common soldier's experiences during the Battle of Gettysburg and, as such, Coco's On The Bloodstained Field is a most necessary reading to anyone with even a passing interest in this country's most celebrated battle.

Robert B. Moore
Hollidaysburg, PA
May 19, 1987

INTRODUCTION

Since the day the Battle ended, people have made their way to the town of Gettysburg to view the scenes of that great struggle. The passage of 124 years has not yet stopped this pilgrimage. The visitors of today, like those of the past, come for varied and contrasting reasons. Some wish to see where the most remarkable event in the Western Hemisphere took place; while others want simply to walk in silence and meditation amid the now quiet fields and woods. There are those, too, who find an interest in Lee's grand strategy, as some study the defensive tactics of the splendid Army of the Potomac. A few view the graves in the Soldiers' National Cemetery and the lingering legacy of Abraham Lincoln's Gettysburg Address as the only true reasons to travel to this world-famous Adams County town. And sadly, there are many who gladly pay homage to the cheap and gaudy "tourist" attractions which are totally unrelated to the terrible and important events which occurred at Gettysburg and probably changed the course of world history.

Nevertheless, whatever your reason for being a part of the million or more travellers who come to this historic place each year, you all have something in common with these countless other and earlier visitors. That common factor is the "human element" present within the story of the Battle of Gettysburg. The simple fact that remains, and should always be remembered, is that *people* fought, suffered, and died here, leaving a rich heritage to be enjoyed and understood by all of us still living. Each of the 150,000 soldiers, and the 2,000 involved civilians was a very *personal* part of the three-day Battle and its aftermath. And all had a story to tell.

Unfortunately, even though human interest stories have been popular battle literature, their number and focus have been somewhat limited in scope. Most, if not all of the publications treating this subject, refer to only a small number of the most commonly known incidents, featuring such famous characters as Jennie Wade, John Burns, Wesley Culp, Henry Wentz, and Generals Barlow and Gordon.

Those long-remembered and oft-repeated narratives are interesting and worthy, in most cases, of being recalled. However, variety is often good, and diversity can and should supplement the old "stand-bys." In On The Bloodstained Field, I have attempted to, in a small way, correct this deficiency.

The accounts, anecdotes, and tales you are about to read have been gathered from hundreds of sources on the Campaign and Battle of Gettysburg. These, and numerous others, were collected while researching material for a book on the field hospitals and wounded associated with that Battle. My purpose in compiling these 130 reminiscences, is to stimulate the imaginations of those who are often overwhelmed by the magnitude of the Civil War, to complement the "hard facts" of the Battle, and to entertain the more knowledgeable students of that War.

Whether you are young or old, male or female, a novice or scholar, you will not miss the point here. These are incidents pertaining to other humans caught up in situations beyond their control. We all, I am sure, can relate to the ghosts within these pages.

As a final note, I would like to say that since none of us living today was in or near Gettysburg during that fearful time, it is impossible to guarantee the legitimacy of all of the memoirs recorded here or anywhere else, for that matter. They are presented here as I found them.

The *majority* of the sources though, to me are as good as can be found in any historical research. Some, of course, may border on the truth, and are obvious. But keep in mind that these incidents most likely occurred as indicated, as did thousands more which were never published, but were kept hidden in the deep recesses of a participant's brain, heart, or soul. A man can seemingly experience a lifetime of thoughts, sights, and sounds in just a few moments confined in the white hot inferno of combat. And, minutes can become years while a soldier dies slowly, lying in a pool of his own blood. Both horror and comedy are often burned into the memory forever — to be passed on later to others, as time slowly heals the jagged scars of war.

Gregory A. Coco
Bendersville, PA 17306
May 4, 1987

PART I

The Campaign: June 15 - June 30, 1863

A Fateful Pair of Shoes

On the march to Gettysburg, members of the 1st Massachusetts Cavalry were ordered to move a sutler's wagon that was obstructing the road. In less than fifteen minutes, the wagon, as well as its contents, were "moved" – every man took any item he wished. Pins, needles, thread, combs, brushes, shoes, tobacco, pipes, etc., were distributed the whole length of the regiment. One fellow got a pair of white canvas shoes. At a halt that night, he took out his pen and ink and wrote his initials, "R.V.C." on the front of each shoe, and put them on to wear.

The next afternoon, while in a severe skirmish with the enemy, this cavalry private was killed. When the regiment fell back, a Rebel saw the shoes and appropriated them to his own use. He did not enjoy wearing them for long, for when the lost ground was retaken, the Reb was found dead, wearing the canvas shoes. Another of the 1st Massachusetts men happily stripped the dead Confederate of the shoes and once more they became Yankee footwear.

On the following day, the fighting began bright and early, and the Southern cavalry was slowly pushed back during the day. Although casualties were light on both sides, one of the first to fall was the Union soldier wearing the white canvas shoes marked "R.V.C."

After that, no one seemed to have a hankering for them, as he was the third man to be killed in them within thirty-six hours.

The Bookworm

A young resident of the town, Sue Myers, witnessed a sight just prior to the Battle which most folks today don't usually associate with "soldiers riding to war." On June 26, the invading Rebels had passed through Gettysburg on their way northward. The next morning Union cavalry came through, and it was a day of rejoicing. Everybody was glad to see them. As they passed through the town, the women hurriedly got anything they could find for them to eat. Sue said, as she was standing in the street helping to pass out provisions, she saw a soldier riding along deeply engrossed in a novel he was reading, and it struck her forcibly to see how composed he was, little knowing whether he would be alive another day.

The Knapsack

On the march into Pennsylvania, a 9th Alabama Infantry soldier witnessed this event as his regiment passed through Chambersburg, and recorded it in his diary.

"*Saturday the 27th* (June). Passed through Marion and Chambersburg. While passing through the latter place Gen'l Lee rode up the column speaking kindly to acquaintances and passed on. The females of Chambersburg seem to be very spiteful, make faces, sing, wave their little banners, etc. A widow in the place discovered the knapsack of her deceased husband in the command. She wished it and the soldier gave it to her. He had picked it up on the battlefield of 'Gaine's Mills,' where we fought the (Pennsylvania 'Bucktails'). Such is war."

A Pass to Heaven

Major Henry Kyd Douglass, a staff officer with the Confederate Second Corps, remembered how General "Stonewall" Jackson, now dead nearly two months, was still loved, even in the midst of the Gettysburg Campaign.

"While we were near Chambersburg a little incident occurred which indicated what a tender memory and stern sense of duty General Jackson had left behind him. Captain Sandy Garber, Assistant Quartermaster of the Second Corps, had been spending the evening in Chambersburg and was returning late at night to his camp. He was halted at the outposts. Having neither pass nor countersign, in his dilemma, he produced an old pass signed by General Jackson from his pocketbook and handed it with great confidence to the sentinel on post. The trusty fellow managed to read it by the light of a match and lingered over the signature. Then, as the light went out, he handed it back and looking toward the stars beyond, he said, sadly and firmly,

"'Captain, *you can go to Heaven on that paper,* but you can't pass this post.'"

Stop the War

When Lee invaded Pennsylvania in late June of 1863, it caused consternation among many of the German or "Dutch" farmers. On one occasion, as a portion of the Confederate army passed across a little stream, one of the artillery pieces became stuck in the creek bottom. Of course, this held up the rest of the column.

On the roadside was a fine field of waving wheat, owned by a local "Dutchman." This wheat was his pride and joy. The fat German farmer came down to the stream to watch the struggle to pull the gun out of the mud. Because of this obstruction, other cannon, men and horses began to go around, cutting across the beautiful field of wheat to reach another ford on the creek higher up.

Naturally, this excited the old farmer, and he became angry. Finding that he was unable by remonstrance to check this tide of invasion through his fine grain, he began to jump up and down crying in a loud voice:

"Mine Gott! Mine Gott in Himmel! If dot is der vay dis var is ter pe carried on, I vants it shtopped righd now!"

The Bare-Bottomed "Bushwack"

A Confederate soldier reported the next story from his experiences in the Gettysburg Campaign.

"It was just before the Battle of Gettysburg and our regiment was camped on the suburbs of a pretty Pennsylvania town. A stream was near the camp, and one afternoon I suggested to some of the boys in my company that we take a bath and a swim. They took to the idea, and likewise to the water, in quick time. There were no houses in the immediate vicinity, except for one on a hillside about half a mile away belonging to an old spinster lady.

"We had been swimming for a while when a boy trudged into camp in search of the captain. He had a note from the old maid, which read:

"*Dear Sir:* I wish you would order your men out of the stream. I can see them plainly through my brother's field glasses!'"

How Devil's Den Was Named

Elizabeth S. Myers, a Gettysburg resident, explains:

"There is another wrong impression which I wish to correct, and that refers to the name of 'Devil's Den.' Many persons have been told that the name was given to those immense rocks because of the fierce fighting there during the Battle of Gettysburg.

"My father's uncle, John Plank, was one of the early settlers of the county, and his farm included a part of the 'Round Tops.' As a child I had heard him tell of the snakes which infested the country, and had their den among those huge rocks. Parties of men were organized to rid the neighborhood of these dangerous reptiles. One big old snake persistently eluded them. They could never kill or capture him and they called him the 'Devil.' He finally disappeared and it was supposed that he died in his den. So, to Gettysburgers that has always been 'Devil's Den.'"

PART II

The Battle: July 1, 1863

Mr. Whisler's Early Morning Scare

Just west of Gettysburg stands a small monument which marks the spot where the first shot of the Battle was fired. On this little ridge stood the house of Ephraim Whisler, a man who was already in his 70's in 1863.

Some time before 8 o'clock on the morning of July 1, a Confederate artillery battery opened up its guns on Union cavalry, which had earlier spotted and fired on advancing Southern infantry. When the firing began, Mr. Whisler hurried out of his house to see what the excitement was all about. As he was peering westward through the smoke and mist, a Rebel cannonball came flying over and landed at his feet! Terribly frightened, Whisler turned and ran back into his home. The shock was so great that he immediately confined himself to his bed – a bed he never left.

Unable to recover from his scare, Ephraim Whisler died a few days later.

The Fifth Alabama and the First Day

William F. Fulton II, of the 5th Alabama Battalion, Archer's Brigade, one of the first men to engage in battle on July 1, saw and heard the following:

"In our advance on July 1, some of our skirmishers passing through a wheat field came to a small cabin, expecting to get behind it as a protection while taking a few shots at some Yankees in the woods beyond. A fierce dog raised an objection – his owner, a shoemaker, came from the cellar, and after commanding his dog to be quiet, inquired, 'What are you here for?'

"He was told a big battle was brewing and we were fixing to take a hand. 'By whom?' he asked. 'By General Lee and the Yankees' was the answer. 'Tell Lee to hold on just a little until I get my cow in out of the pasture,' was his request.

"A little dog had taken up with our company and was a pet with the boys. He was the first fellow shot in our ranks in the first day's battle. He was an innocent bystander, with no concern either way as to which side should whip – yet he was the first struck, and his life was surrendered in the cause of States' Rights and Home Rule.

"(Later) Private Worley, a fine specimen of vigorous young manhood, was carried to the field hospital with an ugly wound in the leg. The doctors said it must come off and prepared to administer chloroform. To this he stoutly objected saying, 'Cut off the leg, Doc, but leave off the chloroform; if you can stand it, I can.'

"He was a brave boy and had done his part nobly in the fight."

The Nameless Heroine

A highly controversial story to come out of the Battle of Gettysburg may or may not have occurred on July 1, but was reported by Lieutenant A.B. Smith of the 76th New York Infantry. He states that many loyal citizens handed out water and food to the passing Union troops.

One, a "nameless heroine," who with a cup in each hand, and tears of sympathy streaming down her lovely cheeks, was pierced by a Rebel ball and fell down beside her water pail. He goes on to say that her name, regretfully, cannot be handed down to posterity.

However, a pension was awarded in 1899 to Lizzie Waltz, a woman who claimed and evidently proved that she was wounded during the Gettysburg Campaign. Lizzie Sweitzer Waltz was a domestic, employed and living in Hanover, Pennsylvania.

John Burns' Wounds

There have been many words written about old John Burns, the Gettysburg constable and ex-veteran of the War of 1812, who was one of the only civilians to act as a volunteer soldier during the Battle. However, even though most of the stories say he was wounded, they universally do not give details of the wounds. Here, from an eyewitness of the Christian Commission, is that information.

"Joining the 7th Wisconsin, he performed a brave man's duty until the close of the first day's battle, when, after being four times hit, he fell into the enemy's hands. His escape with life had been truly marvelous. The first ball struck his side, and was turned away from his body by the intervention of a pair of old-fashioned spectacles in his vest pocket. The second struck a truss worn for an abdominal injury, and glanced off, cutting away the flesh from his thigh about two inches below the top of the hip-bone. The third ball passed through his leg, between the large and small bones without injuring either them or the arteries. The fourth went through the fleshy part of the left arm below the elbow, also without breaking bones or rupturing arteries."

Burns had another close escape from death the next day as he lay resting in bed in his house on the northwest edge of town. A Rebel officer and soldier had come by to question him about the part he had taken in the fight, but Burns made no replies. His window looked out toward a house at some distance, occupied by Confederate sharpshooters. Shortly after the two Rebels left, two balls were fired through his window; one grazed his breast and buried itself in the wall. Only a moment before, the old man, weary of lying on his side turned upon his bed.

On the former position the Minie ball would have passed through his body. Burns always thought it was an assassination attempt in retaliation for the fighting he had done against the Rebels.

The 15 Year-Old "John Burns"

Much has been made, and rightfully so, of the exploits of old John Burns, supposedly the only Gettysburg civilian to take up arms against the invading Rebels. However, another citizen joined the Union ranks on July 1.

This hero was a Maryland boy, about 15 years old, named J.W. (or C.F) Weakley. He tagged along with the 1st Corps from its march through Emmitsburg, all the while begging to join the Union army.

Finally, the veterans of Company A, 12th Massachusetts Infantry, took him in, furnishing young Weakley with a makeshift uniform and weapon. Although never mustered in as a soldier, he fought with the regiment until he was wounded in the arm and thigh. Left on the field, he was cared for by the Confederates. Several months later, Weakley officially joined a U.S. Maryland unit, and was discharged for disability in 1864. His name deserves a proud place in the rich history of the Battle.

One other brave civilian who may have gone out, like John Burns, to meet the Rebels was a Mr. P.A. Branson of Gettysburg. The Star and Sentinel of December 29, 1863, reports that he "behaved valiantly, but was not wounded, and did not receive the notice that Burns did." Branson was a member of the 26th Pennsylvania "Emergency" Regiment and probably fought in a skirmish on June 26. In 1863, he was carried on the tax rolls in Gettysburg as a single man.

The Mississippian

A young orderly, John C. Early, nephew of Confederate General Jubal A. Early, recalled a rebuke he received on July 1 as he tried to find out news of how the Battle was going.

"I, boy-like, was intensely interested in listening to evidences of the fray, when a tall, handsome, bearded officer rode slowly by from the direction in which the fiercest fighting seemed to be going on. I asked him eagerly, 'What news of the fight?' To which he made no reply. On my repeating the question, he still continued silent, but on my third inquiry, he burst out with these words, 'Boy, I am shot through the body and am trying to make my way, before I die, to the Mississippi hospital, and it is hard that in my extremity I should be annoyed by a little whippersnapper like you.'"

Sergeant Stearns Looks Back

Sergeant Stearns recalled two humorous episodes which took place during the Gettysburg Campaign.

"There was an enemy that used to cause the boys considerable trouble and time to keep in a decent state of subjection, and it was no uncommon sight to see many men at the same time engaged in this common warfare. One day while in Pennsylvania, one of the boys had his shirt off 'skirmishing' when an old citizen came along and stopped to look at him while the soldier took no notice. 'Are they Fleas?' said the old citizen. 'Fleas!' said the soldier in a voice of thunder and expressing great indignation. 'What do you take me to be, a damned dog? No, I'm a soldier, and they are *lice*.'"

The other happened to a soldier named Jordan of Company K when the regiment was in full retreat from Oak Ridge on July 1.

"Jordan was retreating at the full run, a Reb in hot pursuit, and had to jump a little brook. The extra exertion caused his only suspender button to come off and his pants falling down tripped him, and he fell head-long into the brook. While he was recovering himself, the Reb came and, laughing at Jordan's predicament said, 'I have a good mind to shoot you.'

"'Shoot,' said Jordan, which increased the Reb's laughter, and he took J. along with him."

The Steel Vest

A popular but soon found to be useless and uncomfortable item purchased early in the Civil War was the steel or "bulletproof" waistcoat. By 1863, these cumbersome vests had mostly been discarded. However, General Jubal Early's nephew, John Early, while serving as a courier at Gettysburg, said that he saw one on the body of a New York officer, probably of the 11th Corps, near a large barn on July 1.

The victim, blonde, about 25 years old, was wearing a solid steel waistcoat. His left arm had been torn off and he had bled to death.

Beside his body were a letter from his bride-to-be and papers for a furlough that was to have begun two days before the Battle.

Brother Captures Brother

Considering the fact that there were over 160,000 men engaged in the Battle of Gettysburg, a remarkable incident occurred on July 1, in the area of Oak Ridge and the Mummasburg Road.

The 45th New York Infantry, which had two companies (A and B) under Captain Korn and Lieutenant Lindemeyer, in a forward position near the McLean barn, captured many Confederate soldiers in and around this prominent red barn. One of the men in Company B was Corporal Rudolph Schwarz. As the Reb prisoners were going to the rear, he recognized his brother in among these defeated Confederates. The brothers embraced right on the spot. They had not seen each other for many years since they both left Germany.

Sadly, Corporal Schwarz of the 45th was killed a short time later as his Reb brother was being marched to the rear as a prisoner.

A Heroic But Selfish Gesture

Captain John Bassler of the 149th Pennsylvania Infantry was wounded in the thigh during the Union Army's hectic retreat on the first day of the Battle. Second Lieutenant Batdorf came to his rescue — but Bassler found it impossible to walk even with this assistance. Batdorf then told him to "get on my back."

As they trotted toward safety, Rebel bullets zipped by, no doubt encouraging Batdorf to even greater efforts with his heavy burden.

Later, within Yankee lines, Lieutenant Batdorf jokingly said that Bassler must not give him too much "credit for disinterestedness; that his object in carrying me on his back was to shield himself from the Rebel bullets!"

An Exciting Escape

Captain Frederick Otto VonFritsch was serving on the staff of Colonel Von Gilsa, 1st Brigade, 1st Division, on July 1 when the 11th Corps was routed and sent flying through Gettysburg to the security of Cemetery Hill.

"I rode behind our men into the town and saw many captured by Grey-coats everywhere." Stopping to speak to a surgeon, VonFritsch was delayed.

"Some twenty Confederates came rushing on, hollaring to me to surrender. One excited fellow got hold of Caesar's bridle with his left hand and was ready to plunge his bayonet into me with his right, screaming: 'Surrender! Get down, you damned Yank!' 'You be damned,' I answered, and cut off his hand with my Saxon sword. Then I started off, gave spurs to my horse, but to my horror found myself in a yard surrounded by high fence rails.

"They shot at me from behind and demanded surrender. Caesar, with an enormous effort, jumped the fence and made off towards Cemetery Hill. Reaching the arch, I dismounted and examined my horse; the poor fellow had been shot twice. My left leg was wounded, my left shoulder strap had been shot away and the shoulder was badly scratched; one bullet had damaged my saddle, and when I tried to replace my sabre, I found the scabbard bent. I had hurt my right knee badly on the fence, and torn off one of my stirrups."

An interesting footnote concerns VonFritsch's sword and horse, Caesar. The sword was of fine Damascus steel. Sharp as a razor, it would bend into a complete circle but never break. It had been inherited from a granduncle who served as a cavalry general under Napoleon the First and who had performed heroic deeds with its aid. His horse, Caesar, was a magnificent bay horse which, during a contest in June 1863, had jumped a five-foot fence with a nine foot ditch behind it! This jump was witnessed by President Lincoln.

The Mysterious Prediction

Lieutenant Colonel John R. Lane of the 26th North Carolina Infantry, after being wounded in the face on July 1, was taken to a brick house that was used as a field hospital. A wounded Georgia officer, who was lying near the door of the room where Colonel Lane lay, had been delirious all morning.

The Georgian finally became quiet about 1:00 p.m., and after a silence of some minutes, Colonel Lane heard him say in a perfectly rational tone of voice: "There now, there now. Vicksburg has fallen, General Lee is retreating and the South is whipped. The South is whipped." He ceased speaking and in a few moments an attendant drew near and said he was dead.

The reader should note that all of these predictions came true several days later, on July 4.

A Fish Story

William Simpson, a drummer in Company A, 28th Pennsylvania Infantry, along with the other musicians of the regiment were gathered together by Surgeon Altman to establish a field hospital. They went over to the Spangler house and, finding it unoccupied, a friend, George McFetridge, went down into the cellar. There, "he found a kit of mackeral . . . and we opened it. We were in for a feast, but we soon found that hardtack and salt mackeral didn't go well together. So Mac took it over to Company K.

"I was in Gettysburg several years later at a reunion, and hunted up the Spangler house. McFetridge was with me. We met the old man at the house and asked him if he missed a kit of mackeral during the battle. 'By jiminy,' he says, 'was you the fellers got the mackeral out of my house? Come in and see my wife.' All excited, he says, '. . . Mom, this is the mens that got the mackeral . . . .'

"Mac and I offered to pay them for it, but they said that they had been reimbursed by the War Department."

A "Nervy" Confederate

This good story was remembered by Tom Hanna, Company F, 83rd New York Infantry, who took refuge in a Gettysburg Lutheran church after being slightly wounded on July 1.

"A little rebel was close beside me – his right arm severely wounded. I fancied that he was not more than 17 years-of-age. He was quite slight in build, and with a counteance and manner effeminate.

"A surgeon examined his arm a moment. 'Immediate amputation,' he said.

"'Fire away,' was the quick reply.

"And I said, with feelings of sympathy mingled with admiration, 'You nervy little Reb.'"

Chaplain Howell's Demise

If you walk from the square about half a block west on Chambersburg Street in Gettysburg, you can't help but notice the beautiful and almost unchanged Christ Lutheran Church on your left. When looking at this wonderful old building, one is thankful it has never been seriously altered. All of the other historic churches in town used as hospitals have been horribly disfigured or replaced, bearing little of their former good taste.

On the lower step of the Christ Lutheran Church is a pretty bronze book-tablet which tells how Chaplain Horatio S. Howell of the 90th Pennsylvania Infantry was killed here on July 1. The impression is that he was *murdered* by Confederates, and in fact most people who know of the incident assume that he, an unarmed non-combatant, was shot down in cold blood. But several other sources point to some altogether different facts.

One regimental account of the 90th Pennsylvania simply says he was "among the killed, falling in the retreat through town . . . . "

Wm. F. Osborn, an assistant surgeon with the 11th Pennsylvania Infantry, recalls: "While going up the church steps with Howell, he turned to look at the Rebel forces as they began entering the town when he was struck in the forehead by one of their bullets and instantly killed."

Mary McAllister, a civilian, remembers six or seven Rebels who came riding up the street firing and yelling. "They halted at the church to say something to the wounded men on the high church steps who had gathered themselves out of range of the firing, and in a few minutes a pistol went off and we saw they had shot a man. The men on the steps said, 'Shame! Shame! That was a Chaplain!"

Jennie McCreary, another civilian, writes on July 22, 1863: "Dr. Parker (13th Massachusetts), was wounded whilst coming down the College Church steps; one of the Rebel sharp shooters fired on him from Boyer's Corner. The same ball that struck him killed the chaplain of that regiment."

The D.C. Chronicle for July 9, 1863, relates how "a squadron of Rebels rode directly up to the front of the (Church) hospital and deliberately discharged their pistols at those on the steps . . . The firing robbed our army of the Rev. Dr. Howell, two privates of New York militia, as well as wounded Dr. Parker of the 13th Massachusetts and Dr. Alexander of the 16th Maine. (The Rebels) seemed exulted over their crimes."

John C. Wills, owner of the Globe Hotel at the time of the Battle, says in his memoirs: "There were already many wounded Union soldiers in the Basement floor and on the second floor of 'Christ's Lutheran College Church' − Rev. Howell had just come out of the Basement floor and was ascending the steps to go up into the second floor. Confederate bullets were coming thick and fast from both ends of the street. He was struck by one of those bullets and killed. (A Union soldier) who was chased up that street by the Confederates said he ran around the corner of Dr. Hill's residence into that Church yard, to shield himself from the rain of bullets, from where he saw the Chaplain fall. Now the tablet at the foot of the steps says he was 'Ruthlessly shot down while kneeling in Prayer.' You form your own conclusion."

Chaplain Howell was born in 1820 in Ewing, New Jersey, studied at Princeton, entered the army in 1861 after having been a pastor at Delaware Water Gap in Pennsylvania, and is now buried in Newark, New Jersey.

The Federal Soldier and Robert E. Lee

Gamaliel Bradford, Jr., recollected meeting the great Southern commander at Gettysburg. As he lay wounded, Lee and some of his staff passed by.

"I recognized him and though faint from exposure and loss of blood, I raised up my hands and shouted, 'Hurrah for the Union!'

"The General heard me, looked, stopped his horse, dismounted, and came toward me. I confess that I thought he meant to kill me. But as he came up he looked down at me with such a sad expression upon his face that all fear left me. He extended his hand to me and, grasping it firmly and looking right into my eyes, said: 'My son, I hope you will soon be well.'

"If I live to be a thousand years, I shall never forget the expression on General Lee's face. As soon as the General had left me, I cried myself to sleep there upon the bloody ground."

The Drink

Late into the night on July 1, columns of Confederate troops continued to march into camps established north and west of Gettysburg. Everyone was exhausted and completely worn out, and the extreme darkness made the marching irregular and very slow. A South Carolina officer recalls a kind act which saved him, *but* put his best friend in an embarrassing situation.

"While marching along at a 'snail's gait' among the wagons and artillery trains, (I noticed) a lone man standing by the roadside viewing, as well as he could in the dark, the passing troops. Just as I was passing him, I heard him say, 'I have a drink in here,' pointing to a tent. Reader, you may have heard of angels' voices in times of great distress? I was so tired, sleepy, and worn out I could scarcely stand, and a drink would be invigorating, but for fear I had not heard clearly, I had him repeat it. After he had, I said, 'Yes! Yes!'

"But just then I thought of my friend and companion, Color Captain John W. Watts, who was just ahead of me and wanted a drink worse than I did. The man answered, 'There is enough for two,' and we went in. It was Egyptian darkness, but we found a jug and tin cups on the table, and helped ourselves. It may have been that in the darkness we helped ourselves too bountifully, for that morning Watts found himself in an ambulance going to the rear. Overcome by weariness and the potion, he lay down by the roadside to snatch a few moments' sleep, and was picked up by the driver of an ambulance as one desperately wounded.

"Just before we went into action that day (July 2), I saw coming through an old field my lost friend, and glad I was to see him, for I was always glad when I had Watts on my right . . . . "

The Rolling Chaplain

A Union chaplain named Eastman was hurt by a plunging horse during the Battle. Unable to walk, he found himself among the wounded. As he lay suffering, he heard a man begin to pray.

"How can I get at him," he wondered. After trying unsuccessfully to walk with the aid of a sapling, he thought, "I can roll." And over and over he rolled in pain and blood, close by dead bodies, until he fell against the dying man – and there he preached Christ and prayed.

Later he was able to secure the help of two soldiers and was carried from one bleeding man to another. At each stop he was laid down unable even to see his audience, where, as he prayed he always looked "heavenward into the eyes of the peaceful stars – emblems of God's love, which even that day of blood had not soiled nor made dim."

Still a Mystery

A strange, almost macabre, incident occurred on West High Street on July 1, in front of the United Presbyterian Church (opposite the Roman Catholic Church). Near the steps at the east end of this church, a soldier who was assisting in the hospital was shot. During the night someone cut off his head, and removed it from the area. No trace of it could be found! Why this was done is unknown, and to this day it is still a mystery.

PART III
The Battle: July 2, 1863

Hampton's Duel

General Wade Hampton, who commanded a brigade under Jeb Stuart, was in position near the village of Hunterstown, a little northeast of Gettysburg, on the morning of July 2. While reconnoitering enemy positions, Hampton heard a bullet suddenly whiz over his head. Turning, he saw the flash of a gun about 300 yards away, then felt another hiss as a second round cut the air near him. He rode at a trot toward the timber to find the hidden sharpshooter. After riding 175 yards, he came to a stake and rider rail fence. Looking to the front he saw a Union cavalryman standing on a large tree stump about 125 yards away. By this time, Hampton was out of sight of his command, but that did not stop him from drawing his .44 cal. revolver and firing. The Yankee fired at the same time. Each man's ball came close but neither was hit. The duel was clearly irregular, but General Hampton held his pistol muzzle up and courteously waited on his antagonist to eject the empty cartridge case and insert a fresh shell into his carbine.

Again, the carbine and pistol blended, and a bullet passed through Hampton's grey cavalry cape, grazing his right breast.

The soldier then reloaded but could not close the breech of his weapon. He raised his right hand with his palm to the front, as if to say 'Wait a bit, I'll soon be with you,' and drew out his cleaning rod and deliberately cleaned out his carbine barrel!

The delay sorely taxed the patience of Hampton, but soon the 'high-roosting cock of the woods' opened fire. But at Hampton's return shot the carbine fell from his grasp and the Yank jumped down and retired to the rear.

Just at that moment the General received a saber blow on the back of his head — he turned on his assailant, who wheeled his horse, and fled at full speed. Hampton followed quickly, his horse springing forward at the touch of the spur.

The fleeing Federal officer who had sabered General Hampton was also well mounted, but Hampton overtook him and leveled his pistol, firing it several times. Each time the percussion cap snapped and the revolver misfired. The Union officer bounded on, but General Hampton had the satisfaction of hurling the pistol at the flying foe, accompanying it with some words which did not entirely become his character as a vestryman of the Protestant Episcopal Church.

NOTE: The cavalryman who was wounded in the wrist was a Michiganer, Private Frank Pearson, and the Federal officer was a lieutenant in the 6th Michigan Cavalry who, years later, met and apologized to General Hampton for his unmanly conduct.

The Apathetic Civilians

Private Henry Berkeley of the Amherst, Virginia, Battery, wrote in his diary on July 2 of an incident involving a Gettysburg family.

"At 9:00 a.m. I was sent with a detail of men to cut down some post and rail fencing around the Pennsylvania College and the town. I cut a great deal of this fencing down.

"In one place, I saw the body of a Yankee which had been cut in two — the head, arms and about one-half of his ribs had been thrown against a fence, and remained with his heart and entrails sticking to the top rail, while some ten feet off, the lower part of the body had been thrown into a mud hole in the road. It was very near a home, and there were three young men in the house.

"I asked these men why they did not bury this body and several others which were near their house, but they would give me no answer."

Mary Elizabeth Finds Her Father

What must have been a tragic encounter was recorded in the diary of a 12 year-old girl, Mary Elizabeth Montfort.

June 8, 1863 – "Today we saw Aunt Beckie. She is a colored lady who helps Mother with the wash. She and some other colored people were pulling wagons or pushing wheelbarrows and carrying big bundles – 'Yo ol' Aunt Beckie is goin' up into de hills. No Rebel is gonna catch me and carry me back to be a slave again.'"

July 1, 1863 – "The soldiers looked tired, dirty, some walked, some rode, but they were dressed in gray. They were Confederate soldiers. Confederate soldiers in Gettysburg."

The next simple entry was made when Mary returned home after caring for the wounded at the railroad station on Carlisle Street.

July (2), 1863 – "Father looked at me and said, 'Mary Elizabeth,' then he closed his eyes. He had been hit by a shell. There was a big hole in his side. Mother told me to go home and take care of Grandma and Jennie Ann. I kissed him once and walked toward the door."

A Reunion

One more story of a soldier meeting his brother, and each in a different army at Gettysburg, occurred on July 2 in the town, which was then held by Southern troops. This incident happened in the rear of the Christ Lutheran Church on Chambersburg Street, and was witnessed by Sergeant Austin C. Stearns, Company K, 13th Massachusetts Infantry, who was a wounded prisoner.

"While out behind the church in the yard cooking our breakfast, there were Rebs and Union men, and there two brothers met, one dressed in blue, the other grey, and with the exception of their uniforms both looked just alike. Both were little, red-faced, red-haired, stubby Irishmen, and both blubbered and cried, and hugged each other as only Irishmen can. The Union man wanted the Reb to go with him and leave the cause of the South, while the Reb didn't see how he could go when the Union man was a prisoner and would perhaps have to go south whether he wanted to or not. How they decided it I never knew, for I left the yard and never saw them again."

The Poisoned Rebels

"At Gettysburg one of our boys of the 134th New York Infantry, observed a number of Rebs lying in an alley apparently very ill. On inquiring the why and wherefore, he found that our erring brethren had got into one of the stores in that place, and obtained something which they imagined was soda which they had used in the manufacture of their biscuits.

"Said *soda* turned out to be *sugar of lead,* and said brethren were taking large rations of emetic and peptic, and such retching, twisting and groaning as those wretches done was enough to melt even the heart of a mudsill."

The Black-Eyed Soldier

Miss Elizabeth S. "Sallie" Myers was a young woman and teacher living on West High Street in 1863. On July 2, she was asked by Surgeon Fulton to assist the wounded in the Catholic Church just east of her home. In 1913, she still remembered:

"Among the first men I saw lying on the floor, to the right of the entrance, were three Southern soldiers. One of them particularly attracted my attention. He was a large man. His complexion was dark, and he had the blackest eyes and hair I ever saw. That was fifty years ago, but today I can see him as distinctly as then, lying there helpless and the appealing look in his great black eyes."

Several weeks later Sallie was at Camp Letterman, the large general hospital east of town, where she entered the "dead tent" to visit several Confederates who were laid out waiting for burial.

"There lay the man who had attracted my attention in the Catholic Church, but the great black eyes were forever closed. On his breast was pinned his name – Hardy Graves (Company C, 6th Alabama Infantry, age 25) – and below it his wife's name and address – Julia Graves, Brundidge, Pike County, Alabama. I cut off a lock of his hair, and sometime after, I wrote to her, sent her the lock and told her what I knew of her husband. She replied and asked me if I could find his grave. He had been buried in a plot of ground along with many others near Camp Letterman. I gathered some wild flowers growing near and enclosed them in a letter, telling her how her husband's grave was situated. I never knew whether Mr. Graves' body was removed (to Richmond) or taken home to Alabama."

General "Wagon Master"

While General Longstreet was marching his corps into position to face the Union left prior to his attack on the afternoon of July 2, a halt was made. The soldiers all fell down exhausted, anxious for some rest. While here, some of General Hill's troops passed by. The head of one particular column was led by a doughty General clad in a brilliant new uniform, a crimson sash encircling his waist, its deep, heavy fringes hanging down to his sword scabbard, while great golden curls hung in maiden ringlets to his very shoulders. His movement was superb and he sat his horse in true knightly manner. He was a sight rarely seen by the staid soldiers of Lee's old First Corps.

As he was passing, a man in Company D, 3rd South Carolina Infantry, roused up from his broken sleep, and saw for the first time this military "wonder" with the long curls. He called out to him, not knowing he was an officer of such rank, "Say, Mister, *come right down out of that hair,*" an expression that was common throughout the army when anything unusual hove in sight.

This hail roused all the ire in the flashy General; he became "mad as a March hare," and wheeling his horse, dashed up to where the challenge appeared and demanded in an angry tone, "Who was it that spoke?" As no reply was given, he turned away, saying, "Damn if I only knew who insulted me, I'd put a ball in him." But as he rode off, the soldier gave him a parting shot by calling out, "Say, Mister, don't get so mad about it, I thought you were some damn wagon master!"

The Irish Woman and the Knife

When Lewis J. Allen, first sergeant of Company F, 1st U.S. Sharpshooters, found himself alone and left behind by his fast retreating comrades on the afternoon of July 2, he bid valor adieu for awhile and broke for the rear. Upon getting out of the woods, he struck plowed ground and here his wind gave out. Sharp pains ran through his side, his long legs refused to go faster than a walk and, all the while, he ran the gauntlet of Southern marksmanship, made more difficult by his sheer exhaustion. Bullets were flying around him, and he expected every moment to be his last. In fact, Allen was just about petered out when he reached a farmhouse where he pushed through the gate and fell exhausted on the green, cool grass. Just then:

"The two women of the house came out. The Irish lady, seeing my convulsive clasp on my side and struggle for breath, ejaculated: 'Lord save us, he's shot!' They ran into the house, crying: 'Where's the butcher knife?' and to my horror, she brought a huge knife like a seaman's cutlass, and began cutting off my belt, knapsack, haversack and canteen. At last I managed to gasp, 'Don't cut any more, I'm not shot!' She fiercely turned with: 'Ye flathering divil ye, ye're making all that divil's fuss and not shot?'

"I looked up to see a squad of Rebs coming through the gate as I had done, and making a hasty grab for my traps that lay as the old lady had strewn them about me, I went out 'on the fly.'"

The Stampede

This particular incident would more likely have happened on a cattle drive from Texas to Kansas in the 1870s, but it occurred on July 2, at Gettysburg, to none other than General Henry J. Hunt, Chief of Artillery of the Army of the Potomac.

After helping to place several guns of Smith's Battery into position near Devil's Den, General Hunt walked off to find his horse so he could ride for infantry supports to assist the battery. But Confederate artillery opened just then and shells began to fall all through the area. Hunt explains:

"On reaching the foot of the cliff, I found myself in a plight at once ludicrous, painful, and dangerous. A herd of horned cattle had been driven into the valley between Devil's Den and Round Top, from which they could not escape. A shell had exploded in the body of one of them, tearing it to pieces; others were torn and wounded. All were *stampeded*, and were bellowing and rushing in their terror, first to one side and then to the other, to escape the shells that were bursting over them and among them. Cross I must, and in doing so I had my most trying experience on that battlefield. Luckily the poor beasts were as much frightened as I was, but their rage was subdued by terror, and they were good enough to let me pass through scot-free, but 'badly demoralized.' However, my horse was safe; I mounted, and in the busy excitement that followed almost forgot my scare."

A Sad Day for Mother

M.V.B. Sutton, who served in Company K, 18th North Carolina Regiment, wrote in 1914:

"On the second day's fight at Gettysburg, in the early morning, Longstreet's or A.P. Hill's men were moving down to our right and the Yankees commenced shelling us, so we lay down to protect ourselves.

"I belonged to the pioneer corps of our regiment. During the cannonading a shell missed me about a foot, plunged into the ground, and exploded directly underneath three soldiers who were lying down, throwing them at least ten feet in the air and killing them instantly.

"As soon as it was safe to do so, I took the men under my command and cleaned out the hole that the shell had made, wrapped the bodies in some blankets, and buried them there. While so occupied, I looked up and saw a soldier standing beside the grave, and I said to him:

" 'I am doing the best I can for them.' He replied: 'I see you are.' I then asked if he knew them, and he answered: 'Yes, my brothers.'

"I wanted to ask their names, but when I looked up again he was gone."

John M. and the Scythe

John Morrison was a farm boy employed in 1861 on a large farm in Bradford, Massachusetts. One day while cutting grass leisurely in a field, he decided he could put off the decision no longer. He must enlist! At that moment he impulsively thrust the scythe he was mowing with under a swath of grass, and leaving it there, walked off to tell his employer of his decision.

After joining the 22nd Massachusetts Infantry, John became a great favorite. His peculiar appearance, his quaint manner, and strict adherence to duty, his irresistible way of telling a story, a strong nasal twang predominating, won for him many friends.

The story of the scythe leaked out and from that time on became a standing joke. On every hard, exhausting march, or tedious trying duty, John was always sure to be hailed by every Company H member with, "Well, John, where is the scythe? Don't you wish you was swinging her this morning? That scythe will surely rust, John, before you go home!" To which came the invariable reply, "The scythe is under the swath in the field. I don't want to do any mowing today. Let her rust! *Rather be here!*"

On the long, dusty, hot and terribly depressing march to Gettysburg, the army was so exhausted, troops were straggling by the hundreds. Every face looked like leather, be-streaked with sweat and dust. In the quiet misery of that long afternoon, the question was asked of John: "Well, John, how *would* that scythe go today?" John's face came up white and ghostly. There was no twinkle of the eye or comical smile, while he quietly and with sub-dued voice said, "*Yes,* I wish I could swing her today."

All noticed his manner, the sober delivery, devoid of spirit. The joke was hushed, all wondering about John Morrison.

On July 2, when the 22nd met the fire of Longstreet's advancing Rebel columns on a rocky ridge northwest of Round Top, John was shot through the body while loading and firing his musket at the enemy. Later his comrades saw his white and pain contorted face and heard his cry of, "Lay me down to die." He was shot through the bowels and died in the 11th Corps Hospital on the Spangler farm, and was buried in the National Cemetery in a grave marked unknown.

The Altar Stone

A story was written in the Atlantic Monthly about a colonel leading his regiment in a charge at Gettysburg, shouting to them in a rich and hearty voice, "Come on men, come on, you are all good harvesters, and the grain is ripe!" As the regiment reached a line of boulders the colonel sprang upon one shaped like a large flat altar stone. Upon it, outstretched, face upward, in a pool of blood, lay a young lieutenant who had been killed on the skirmish line a quarter hour before. "Come on, come on," the colonel cried as suddenly he faced the dead man.

The oncoming line of his men saw him stand as if frozen, then with a stiff jerk, up went his sword again. "Come on, come on," he yelled as he plunged ahead toward the desired slope. His men, close behind, also encountered the dead officer. "Good God! It's the Lieutenant! *His son!* "

But in front they still heard the colonel's voice, "Come on!"

Scare Tactics

When the 148th Pennsylvania Infantry was fighting in the Wheatfield at Gettysburg on July 2, one soldier made this observation:

"Men in battle will act very differently; some become greatly excited, others remain perfectly cool. One of the boys in my rear was sitting flat on the ground and discharging his piece in the air at an angle of forty-five degrees, as fast as he could load.

"'Why do you shoot in the air?' I asked.

"'To *scare* 'em,' he replied."

Lt. Oliver, C.S.A., Saves Lt. Purman, U.S.A.

After assisting one of his men in the Wheatfield during the fighting on July 2, Lieutenant Jackson J. Purman, 140th Pennsylvania Infantry, was shot in the left leg attempting to retreat to Union lines. After falling to the ground, he received another wound through his right leg. Unable to crawl off, he lay under the fire of both armies throughout the night and into the next day. Hailing a Confederate officer, Lieutenant Thomas P. Oliver, 24th Georgia Infantry, Purman asked for help. Oliver, in the midst of deadly volleys, dragged Purman to safety and left him with a canteen of water.

Several days later, Purman was taken to the house of the Witherow family in Gettysburg. He was nursed by one of the girls of the family, Mary, whom he later married. After the War, he was able to locate Oliver, who became a fast friend and correspondent until 1908 when Lieutenant Oliver died in Athens, Georgia.

The Cherry Picker

While the 12th New Hampshire Infantry was supporting a battery in an orchard near the Emmitsburg Road at Gettysburg, one of the boys of Company E climbed into a cherry tree, the better to help himself to the tempting fruit thereon. Though he went up nimbly like a live squirrel, he came down like a dead possum, to the great amusement of his comrades, when they found that the solid shot cannonball that brought him down had more frightened him than hurt him. He was quite unable to tell whether the limb he stood on was cut off, or *he* knocked off the limb. His own version of the affair put into rhyme is very brief, but expressive:

> I heard something snap, and I felt something 'drap' –
> Make no queries;
> For th' next thing I knew I had got all through
> Picking cherries.

A Horrible Death

"Explosive bullets" were used by some regiments during the Civil War. These bullets were implanted with a powder train and a small explosive charge was placed in the nose of the bullet. These bullets exploded soon after being fired and, if embedded inside a man's body, caused terrible havoc.

Prior to Gettysburg, the 2nd New Hampshire Infantry had been issued some of these bullets. However, in the case of one soldier, the user became the victim.

During the fighting at the Peach Orchard on July 2, "several cartridge boxes were exploded. A shell struck and burst on the box of Corporal Thomas Bignall of Company C. The (explosive) cartridges were driven into his body and fired, and for nearly half a minute the devilish 'musket shells' were exploding in his quivering form. But death was mercifully quick.

"The next moment a fragment of shell exploded the cartridge box of Sergeant J.M. House of Company I. The rapidity with which he tore off the infernal machine hanging by his side was astonishing, and he escaped with only a severe wound."

Out of the Ambulance and into the Fight

A member of the New Jersey Brigade upon his arrival in the rear of the Union lines at Gettysburg recorded an incident he stated he would never forget.

It was that of a very ill soldier climbing out of an ambulance, shouldering his musket, and starting forward. The surgeon in charge of the ambulance train stopped him and asked, "Where are you going, sir?"

"To the front, Doctor," said the brave fellow as he tried hard to stand firm and speak boldly.

"To the front! What! A man in your condition? Why, Sir, you can't march half a mile; you haven't the strength to carry yourself, let alone your knapsack, musket, and equipments. You must be crazy surely."

"But, Doctor, my division are in the fight, and I have a young brother in my company. I *must* go."

"But I am your surgeon, and I forbid you. You have every symptom of typhoid fever; a little over-exertion will kill you."

"Well, Doctor, if I *must* die, I would rather die in the field than in an ambulance."

The Doctor saw it was useless and the soldier went as he desired.

On the evening of the next day the eyewitness to the above scene had to bury this brave man where he had fallen. His right arm was blown off at the elbow, and his forehead had been pierced by a Minie ball.

The Dying Hero

The Second Division of the 5th Corps was going to the rear, taking many of their wounded with them.

One man, who was supported by two comrades, had had his lower jaw blown off, and as he moved along, held up in his hand the bloody bone, misshapen and splintered, with nine teeth still remaining in it. Another, lying upon a stretcher, had lost both feet by a solid shot. The bleeding stumps had not been dressed, and the stretcher was covered with the blood of the dying hero.

Yet for all this, amid the roar of musketry, and with the pain his wound must have caused, he was singing in a clear voice, with enough of the Irish accent to make the strain musical:

> The Star-Spangled Banner, oh long may it wave
> O'er the land of the free and the home of the brave.

The Drummer

The sight of a little drummerboy attracted my attention.

In a childish voice, as he held up his left arm from which the hand had been severed, while he held his drum with the other, he said, "Will *you* do as much as that for the Union?"

"Yes, my little fellow, if I must."

"Well, I'll do more," and he held up his good hand; "but then, I would have no hands at all to work for mother, and father was killed at Antietam."

I should suppose, from the little fellow's appearance, he was not over twelve or thirteen years of age; he was a young hero, but a thorough one – a child worthy of the Republic, worthy of its inspirations, worthy of the future in which, maybe, he shall sit crowned with honors.

An Unexpected Bath

One of the drivers of the Ambulance Corps was stooping on a log washing his hands in a small creek just in the rear of the Federal line of battle. A spent shell came ripping through the trees behind him and buried itself just deep enough in the log to make it stick. The driver turned about and with the heel of his boot kicked the shell into the water, saying: "Now, old screech owl, bust if you want to."

And burst it did, only a second or two after, blowing one end of the log into splinters and completely deluging the driver.

Dropping himself astride the remainder of the log, he surveyed himself coolly and exclaimed, "Well, I came here to wash my hands, but hang me if I expected a shower-bath in such an out of the way place as this."

A Company Is Drilled under Fire

"A remarkable instance of coolness under fire was exhibited in the midst of the Battle by Lieutenant James Doherty, 1st Massachusetts Infantry, who, observing that his company was a little tremulous, ordered them to bring their guns to their shoulder.

While the Rebel battle-front was aflame with deadly volleys, and a perfect tornado of whizzing missiles was flying at, over, and among his men, he put them through the manual of arms as quietly as he would in front of their quarters in camp."

Killed by a Shell that Never Struck

There are accounts of soldiers who were killed or died in battle without being struck. One such example occurred in the 57th Pennsylvania Infantry on July 2. It was this way.

"The men that had started ahead of me were following up the regiments in an irregular form . . . and shells were dropping very close to me. A man in front was in range and (I) feared one would strike him . . . but instead it just missed him, but he dropped as dead and limp as though his head had been cut off.

"I know he was not touched, for I rolled him over, and there was no bruise on his head or face."

Adams County Milk

Robert McAllister, colonel of the 11th New Jersey Infantry, was wounded on July 2 in the late part of the afternoon. He was carried to the rear and was looked after by Dr. Welling. Even though most of his acquaintances knew he did not use alcohol, the doctor urged him to take a little whiskey to stimulate his waning strength. Colonel McAllister, however, steadily refused. Dr. Welling, then, without his knowledge, prepared an appetizing milk punch with some of the whiskey, which McAllister readily drank.

He was heard long afterwards speaking in terms of praise of the milk given by the Gettysburg cows.

The Angry Captain

Twenty years later, Colonel Powell, of the 5th Texas Infantry, could still remember many things concerning his captivity behind Union lines during the second and third days of the Battle.

"When first taken over the lines, I was temporarily placed near a Captain White, a Union officer, who had been posted in our front. During the fight he had held a flag near or on the works, and one of the Texans, seeing him, determined to have that flag. He got it, but the Captain held on to the staff although he seemed to be stuck full of holes by a bayonet; his hands and arms were literally torn to pieces. I think he was the maddest man I ever saw and said he would have given a hundred lives rather than have lost that flag. The Captain and myself were informed by the surgeon that we were both mortally wounded.

"But we have met since and fought that battle o'er."

Colonel Powell Recalls

Other incidents passed before Colonel Powell's eyes on that long suffering July day.

"We had an agreeable visit from some cavalry officers. A colonel who said he was from Rochester, New York, and was known as 'Dare-Devil Dick,' gave us substantial and invigorating comfort which he carried in a flask.

"The recognition of two brothers was a circumstance of greater surprise than pleasure – one, a staff officer in the Union army, and the other, a wounded Confederate. The loyal brother essayed a little speech of censure and reproach, which the Confederate promptly discouraged by saying with emphasis that he was competent to decide and act for himself. Colonel 'Dare-Devil Dick' interrupted the controversy by saying it was not the time or place for such talk.

"We were visited by several members of the 14th U.S. Regulars, whom we had met on our bloody excursion up Little Round Top. They said we had almost destroyed them. They were Georgians and, like hundreds of other young fellows, had fallen into disgrace at home, and had enlisted in the (U.S.) Army just before the war. They said they did not take any stock in patriotism or glory but, being in on *that* side they proposed to stay."

Panty Raid

Toward evening on July 2, a Confederate officer rode out to the Cunningham farm to tell the owner that his barn would be required for hospital purposes. All night long the wounded were carried in on stretchers and by morning the barn and orchard nearby were filled with Union and Confederate men who had been hurt fighting around the Wheatfield.

Later in the day, a man came running to the house demanding that Mr. Cunningham give him something red to be used as a hospital flag. The Rebels were retreating, he said, and the area would be shelled – a flag would offer some safety to the hospital.

Cunningham's daughter explains what happened next:

"Father was not a handy man about the house. He opened a drawer and handed out the first thing he touched. It was white, not red, but the haste was great. In a few minutes this white thing was floating from the lightning rod of the barn. When Mother came back from Grandfather's, this was the first spot that caught her eye – a pair of her nether garments gleaming high against the blue sky! And those garments could not, with truth, be called 'scanties' in 1863."

Private Chase's Long Journey Home

Twenty year-old John F. Chase, a private in the 5th Maine Battery, was with his unit atop a knoll between Cemetery and Culp's Hills on the evening of July 2, when Louisiana and North Carolina troops assaulted Cemetery Hill. He recalls this unusual adventure:

"My battery was enfilading the charging column as it dashed up the hill. Our shot,

shrapnel, and canister was doing such terrible execution that the Confederates opened three or four batteries on us.

"One of their shrapnel shells exploded near me and 48 pieces of it entered my body. My right arm was shattered and my left eye was put out. I was carried a short distance to the rear as dead, and knew nothing more until two days after.

"When I regained consciousness, I was in a wagon with a lot of dead comrades being carted to the trenches to be buried. I moaned and called the attention of the driver, who pulled me up among the dead, and gave me water. He said my first words were: 'Did we win the battle?'

"I was taken to the First Army Corps Hospital on the Isaac Lightner farm, three miles from Gettysburg on the Baltimore Turnpike. They laid me down beside the barn, where I waited three more days before my wounds were dressed. The surgeon let me lie there to 'finish dying,' as they said, while they attended to the rest of the wounded. I lay on the barn floor then, several days, and then was taken into the house, where I stopped for a week. From there I was removed to the Lutheran Theological Seminary Hospital.

"After about three weeks, I was carried out of the hospital to die again, and was told by the head surgeon that I could not live six hours, but I did not do him the favor. Three months later, I was sent to West Philadelphia Hospital until I was able to return to my home in Augusta, Maine."

NOTE: Chase won the Medal of Honor for his bravery at Chancellorsville, in May 1863.

The "Tiger" Asks for Quarter

Sometimes in the heat of battle, men become overzealous with inflicting injury to the enemy, as in this incident which happened on Cemetery Hill in the evening on July 2 during a Confederate attack on Union artillery holding that position.

"A Sergt. of the (Louisiana) 'Tigers' got clear back to the limbers, and there caught Private Riggins' horse, and picked up (our) fallen colors. While leading back the horse he was encountered by Sergt. Stratford, who, unable to recognize him in the dark, demanded to know where he was going with that horse. The rebel immediately brought his musket to his shoulder and demanded Stratford's surrender.

"At this moment I walked up and a glance showed me the true state of affairs. Having no sidearms by me, I picked up a stone, and in a most unmilitary manner broke the fellow's head. He tumbled to the ground, but Stratford not knowing the cause seized the musket and shot him through the abdomen. Fearing he had missed him in the darkness, he clubbed the musket and broke the fellow's arm, whereupon he asked for 'quarter,' which, of course, was given.

"I don't think he lived long."

A Frightful Encounter

During the evening of July 2, Captain Charles H. Weygant made his way to a field hospital in the rear in search of men of the 124th New York who had been wounded earlier in the day. A most hideous scene greeted his eyes and ears.

"The scene at the hospital was one of the most horrid imaginable. During the afternoon and evening nearly 3,000 wounded men had been brought there. The ground of the entire grove, several acres in extent, seemed to be literally covered with them; and such noises filled the air as I had never heard before and trust may never reach my ears again. I resolved to attempt to pick my way through, toward where I hoped to find the objects of my search . . . .

"Presently a man I was about stepping over, sprang to his feet, shook in front of me a bloody bandage he had just torn from a dreadful gaping wound in his breast, and uttered a hideous laughing shriek which sent the hot blood spurting from his wound into my very face; at which he threw up his arms as if a bullet had just entered his heart, and fell heavily backward across a poor mangled fellow whose piercing wails of anguish were heart-rending beyond description.

"I could endure no more . . . . "

The Twelfth Battle

Just before the Battle of Gettysburg, Sergeant Edward B. Rollins of Company A, 15th Massachusetts Infantry, sent a card to his wife with the name of eleven battles he had fought, beautifully inscribed upon it. He left space for inscribing one more name, and wrote to her that after he had fought his twelfth battle he would come home.

He was killed at Gettysburg on July 2 — his twelfth battle.

A Woman Doctor?

Did the Confederates have a woman doctor in service at Gettysburg? If so, it is truly one of the most carefully kept secrets of that conflict. And even though the services of Dr. Mary Walker, a Union surgeon who worked with the wounded here, are not so well known, the presence of a Rebel woman surgeon is even more astounding. Here is how Lizzie R. (Plank) Beard got suspicious.

"Here is a true story of the happenings on the (Edward Plank) farm about three miles west of Gettysburg, situated on the west bank of Willoughby's Run. The house is a large brick . . . the family consisted of three small children, the parents, and an uncle. On July 1, we were told, 'This house will be a hospital and you can expect many wounded men here.'

"At this hospital, there were two Doctors, one a very well built man of fine personality. (His) name cannot be recalled. The other – John R. Bodly of Georgia – was a smaller man of kind disposition and bore the many characteristics of a woman, and was often spoken of, by the family as 'the Woman Doctor.' These two doctors were constant companions. One winter I read in one of the New England papers of a woman, I can't recall her name, and the story in full of her enlisting and being in the service during the Battle of Gettysburg. I don't say John R. Bodly was this woman, but this clipping goes a long way to prove that there was a woman doing service after the Battle at a Gettysburg hospital."

PART IV
The Battle: July 3, 1863

The Old Crone

Somewhere along the Baltimore Pike near Culp's Hill, the 3rd Wisconsin Infantry noticed an old woman standing on the side of the road, her "arms akimbo, resting on her broad hips, and she spoke words of cheer to us, such as these: 'Dot ish right, poys, go and drive dose fellows off. De has shtole enough around here!' She was the same old crone whom Colonel Morse records that when the 2nd Massachusetts Infantry was moving across the turnpike to the left on the night of the 2nd, while the Rebels were yelling like devils incarnate, she said to their men, 'Never mind, poys, they're nothing but *MEN*.' She was a woman of superb nerve, and her words amused and encouraged the men in that hour of high excitement."

Toothache!

Amid all of the terrible carnage and suffering that went on during the Battle of Gettysburg, one lieutenant had the ignominious misfortune to suffer a toothache on July 3.

"I received permission to go back to the hospital, to get an ugly tooth extracted that had kept me dancing all the night before. Our Surgeon, Dr. Everett, who had been hard at work all night at the amputation table, made but short work and little ado about one tooth. He laid me on the ground, straddled me, and with a formidable pair of nippers pulled and yanked me around until either the tooth had to come out, or my head off. I was glad when the head conquered."

The Heroism of Abner Webb

On July 3, Captain Silas Gardner of Company C, 3rd Wisconsin Infantry, witnessed an act of heroism as daring as any performed during the War.

"After regaining our works on (Culp's Hill) we found quite a number of the enemy in and in front of the breastworks. Our lines were very close together at this time – so close that if you wanted your hat ventilated, all you had to do was to put it on a stick and be careful not to put your head in it, and raise it above the works. There was an open piece of ground about 50 or 75 yards in front, where a number of the killed and wounded lay. The day was very hot, and there was one man among the wounded who commenced calling for water. I have heard that cry many times before and since, but nothing like that one. (He had) an entreaty and pathos in his voice that would touch a heart of stone. It was maddening. The men all became nervous, would move uneasily about, and tried to keep up conversation, but still that cry rang out.

"Soon I saw a member of my company spring to his feet, hasten to the rear and fill his canteen from the spring, come back and take off his accoutrements. It was Abner Webb. I asked him what he was going to do. He replied: 'Captain, I can't stand it any longer, I am going to take that man a drink if they shoot the hell out of me.' I called the men into line, and as we sprang over the works, we opened fire, but they did not seem to pay much attention to us, but directed their fire to the unarmed (Abner Webb). He reached the wounded man, and throwing himself on the ground beside him, raised the canteen to the lips of the sufferer and let him drink. After breathing himself a moment, leaving the canteen, he started on the return trip. The bullets of the enemy fairly rained around him, even though they could plainly see what he had done. But through that storm of lead he sprang over the works untouched.

"With a cheery smile on his face he said, 'Well, I gave him a drink in spite of them.'"

A Rebel Commits Suicide

Captain Moore recalls:

"It was about 11 o'clock a.m. when Johnson's Rebel Division . . . with astonishing deliberation moved on our position. The 147th Pennsylvania Infantry and the troops on its right and left very calmly withheld their fire until the enemy came within easy rifle range. The enemy advanced steadily (and) reached a distance of less than 100 yards from our position, when (we) poured a deadly fire into their ranks; the destruction of the Rebel column was almost complete.

"Only one stalwart Rebel was left standing among the mass of killed and wounded. Another wounded man in our front was observed laying on his back reloading his gun, and our men, surmising that he intended to shoot at them raised their guns to dispatch him.

"The wounded Rebel then deliberately placed the muzzle of his gun under his chin, and with his ramrod forced the trigger and shot himself through the head."

Honorably Buried

Brigadier General Thomas Kane tells this story of the Culp's Hill fight in a letter dated March 21, 1874:

"A pet dog belonging to a company of the 1st Maryland (Confederate) charged with the regiment, ran ahead of them when their progress was arrested, and came in among the Boys in Blue. At first he barked in valorous glee, but (later) I saw him on three legs going between our men, and the men in Gray on the ground, as though looking for a dead master, or seeking to find an explanation of the tragedy he witnessed. He licked some-one's hand after being perfectly riddled with bullets.

"Regarding him as the only Christian-minded being on either side, I ordered him to be honorably buried."

The Bravest Act

In the 2nd Corps Hospital, one of the most pathetic incidents of the war occurred.

A young soldier, a mere boy, was brought in on a stretcher while a soldier walked alongside and held his hand on a wound in the thigh of the boy's body. He said he was entirely free from pain. A surgeon examined the wound and said, "Nothing can be done for you; you must die; if you have any word or message to send home, attend to it at once; you will die within a few moments after your comrade takes his hand from your wound, and that must be soon."

The soldier asked for paper and pen which were quickly furnished. He wrote a letter to his mother, stated his condition and that a friend was holding the wound while he wrote to her, saying as soon as he finished the letter his comrade would let go and he would bleed to death in a few minutes.

The letter was finished, he let himself fall back, hesitated a moment, then said, "Now you may let go," and Levi Smith, of Company A, 148th Pennsylvania Infantry, who held the wound, withdrew his hand, and in a few minutes, life had gone out.

General Hancock and the Little Girl

General Winfield S. Hancock, commander of the Union Second Corps at Gettysburg, came upon a child who was only six years old or so, while passing near the outskirts of his lines just before Pickett's famous charge. She was hardly able to speak plainly. The little girl somehow had strayed near the pickets, bringing an old rifle that was heavier than the child could carry. When she saw General Hancock, she held the load in her arms, crying, "My papa's dead, but here's my papa's gun." There was a tear in General Hancock's eye as he recited this heroic incident. "I never recall that brave chit of a child's offering to our cause," he said, "without feelings of deepest reverence. Her half-lisped words voiced a sentiment that was sublime."

Run for Cover

On July 3, a colonel of Hood's Division was lying wounded near the stone house of an aged German and his wife. Everything was quiet during the morning hours. Soldiers and surgeons went about their duties in a lazy summertime way; the old German sat on the doorstep in meditative silence, smoking some imported tobacco, his wife was tending the chickens she had hidden in the loft.

"Suddenly without threat or warning, like a clap of thunder in a clear sky, a storm of shot, shrieking shell, and the roar of 200 cannon seemed to fill all space above the trembling earth.

"The old German promptly took refuge in the well and, 'we knew by the smoke which so gracefully curled,' that his pipe was the companion of his fear. The old wife left her chickens to look after Fritz. The treacherous smoke betrayed his hiding place. We thought she intended to join him in the well, but to our surprise she seemed unconscious of danger from the flying missiles. (She) danced around the well frantically imploring him to come out. She said he would 'die mit cold.' He only replied, 'Mine Got, Katrine! Nein, Nein!'"

A Morbid Joke

While lying under the terrific bombardment preceding Pickett's Charge on July 3, Corporal Simon Hubler, Company I, 143rd Pennsylvania Infantry, saw a man crawl up beside him. The soldier explained that a shell had just struck a man in Company D of their regiment, taking off his head just above the ears, and scattering his brains over seven other soldiers.

Just then a man by the name of Stair called over, "Did it kill him?"

Hubler said that "the boys roared with laughter" and called Stair a fool.

A Wounded Horse

There were literally thousands of horses and mules killed or wounded during the three-day Battle of Gettysburg. Their suffering is often overlooked. One animal's terror was remembered by a veteran.

"Suddenly a cry of horror breaks from the group of wounded . . . . A wounded horse at a mad gallop comes tearing straight toward them. His ironclad hooves strike the ground . . . . A cannon shot has torn through his lower jaw, leaving it hanging by a few shreds. With head thrown high in the air, uttering frenzied cries of pain, the severed jaw swinging and whirling at every stroke of the hoofs, his magnificent white breast covered with the spouting blood, he plunges straight toward the score or more of mangled human beings. 'Shoot him! Shoot him!' goes up from many a lip . . . . "

Finally, luckily, the horse swerved from his course and passed into the trees.

The Furrow

At one point during the great artillery duel at Gettysburg, the men of Company G of the 17th Mississippi Infantry were pinned down in a cornfield, and every man was lying as low as he could among the rows of corn. One soldier, Lee Hill, of that company is reported to have broken the tension by crying out –

"Damn a man who won't plow a furrow deeper than this!"

To Err Is Human

At Meade's headquarters (Lydia Leister's House), during the cannonade on the afternoon of July 3, a staff officer saw his horse become badly wounded by a piece of shell. He ran into the house to get his pistol to put the horse out of its misery.

Coming out in a terrible hurry, he "put two bullets into a fine *uninjured* horse belonging to Captain Hall, signal officer of the Second Corps . . . !"

Slocum's Rage

"It was at the Battle of Gettysburg when the bullets were falling like hail, and the shells were shrieking and bursting over our heads in a way to make the bravest heart tremble.

"A private dropped out of the ranks and skulked back to the rear. He was well under way when, unfortunately for him, he was met by General Henry W. Slocum coming to the front.

"'What are you doing here? Get back to your post,' the General shouted to the Twelfth Corps soldier.

"The poor fellow stopped still and trembled like a leaf, but made no reply.

"'Get back to your post, you miserable coward; aren't you ashamed of yourself, to be back here when you should be with your brave comrades?'

"Still the man made no reply, but commenced to cry like a year-old infant.

"'You infamous, sneaking coward,' shouted the infuriated General, 'get back to your post; I'll ride you down like a dog. Why, you are nothing but a baby.'

"'I-I-I'll t-t-tell you what, G-g-general,' said the blubbering fellow, 'I'd g-g-give anything just n-n-now if I was a b-b-baby, and i-i-if I had my ch-ch-choice I'd r-r-rather be a female b-b-baby!'"

His Son Fell

In the official report written on July 9, 1863, by Major C.S. Peyton, 19th Virginia Infantry, Garnett's Brigade, is a sad reminder of the terrible cost of war and the courage it takes to endure its vulgarity. The following happened during Pickett's Charge on July 3.

"The conduct of Captain M.P. Spessard of the 28th Virginia was particularly conspicuous. His son fell mortally wounded at his side; he stopped but for a moment to look on his dying son, gave him his canteen of water, and pressed on with his company to the wall, which he climbed, and fought the enemy with his sword in their own trenches until his sword was wrested from his hands by two Yankees; he finally made his escape in safety."

Where Is the Colors?

One of the men who crossed the wall at the Angle with Armistead was Calvin P. Dearing, Company G, 28th Virginia Infantry, who lived after the war in Kentucky.
"The Yankees were surely very nice to us," he noted. "They didn't shoot at us after we got into their lines, but just told us to surrender, and we did.
"Colonel Allen was my colonel and he came from the same county I did. They laid him and me together, and he took his hat off a little and he said, 'Dearing, where is the colors?' Then he put his hat back on his head and died right then."

The Last Words of Sumner Paine

Sumner Paine, the great-grandson of a Revolutionary War patriot, was born in Boston on May 10, 1845. By the time he was twelve, Sumner had already spent a year touring Europe. And when the Civil War was four months old in July of 1861, young Paine entered Harvard College, at the ripe old age of sixteen. Having a strong desire to be a part of the great struggle, Sumner joined the army in May of 1863 as a Second Lieutenant in the 20th Massachusetts Infantry. Due to the wounding of his captain, Oliver W. Holmes, Lieutenant Paine led his company into the Battle of Chancellorsville, within 24 hours of receiving his commission. By all reports, his behavior was extremely cool and calm through that terrible fight.

Exactly two months later on July 3, 1863, Lieutenant Paine was standing with his men on Cemetery Ridge, when the 20th Massachusetts met the assault head on of Confederate Generals Pickett, Pettigrew and Trimble. It was in the thickest of the fray that Paine, exposing himself directly in front of his men, was hit by a rifle ball which broke his leg. Falling on one knee, he waved his sword, and urged his men on, calling out: *"Isn't this glorious?"* A moment later, he was struck by a shell which caused instant death.

If you have time, walk to the Soldiers' National Cemetery and stand for a few minutes at his grave. Here you may wish to contemplate a young man's short but noteworthy life. Imagine, if you can, what he might have accomplished had he lived another 50 or 60 years.

A Pennsylvania Civilian in Pickett's Charge

J.F. M'Kenrick of Ebenburg, Pennsylvania, wrote the following story to Confederate Veteran Magazine in 1911.
"I was not a Confederate veteran in the sense that an enlistment would imply, but it was my singular fortune to participate with Pickett's Division from daylight on July 3 until dawn of July 4, 1863. Living at that time near Cashtown and anxious to witness the Battle, I went into the ranks of Kemper's Brigade and was permitted to accompany it to its position on the field.
"When the division went into action, I followed as a volunteer, and participated with the ambulance corps in caring for the wounded, saw the advance, repulse, and retreat . . . . In that single day I saw enough to satisfy my boyish curiosity.
"Forty-seven years later it was my pleasure to meet the widow of the hero, General Pickett, whose name is so intimately associated with that reminiscence of my life."

The Dedicated Color Sergeant

The Color Sergeant of the 16th Vermont fell mortally wounded during a flank attack on Kemper's Brigade on July 3. At once a dozen men rushed forward. The poor wounded sergeant grasped the staff with both his clenched hands, his eyes already dimmed with death. He could not see who it was that tried to wrest his charge from him. "Are you friends or enemies?" he cried out.
"We are friends," was the reply, "give us the colors." "Then, friends," said he, "I am mortally wounded, let me hold up the flag till I die."
And so saying, he fell back . . . dead.

A Shocking Discovery

George Hale Scott, a sergeant in Company G, 13th Vermont, searching the field after Pickett's Charge, found a Union officer finely dressed and leaning against a tree with his hat pulled over his face. Not knowing if the officer was sleeping or dead, Scott lifted the hat and saw that the man's head was gone!

Musketry Fire

The following illustration may give the Gettysburg visitor an idea of how terrific the musketry fire could get in certain places during the Battle. From the evidence, it is a wonder anyone could have survived such fire.

"On the Emmitsburg Road, (the slab fences) were so completely perforated with bullet holes that you could scarcely place a half inch rule between them. One 1¼ inch thick board was indeed a curiosity. It was 16 feet long, 14 inches broad and was perforated with 836 musket balls. This board was on that part of the fence where Scale's brave little brigade crossed it."

Arkansas Sharpshooters

Almost everyone who visits the National Military Park at Gettysburg, and tours the Little Round Top or Devil's Den areas will undoubtedly hear something of the "sharpshooting" which went on between both sides there. Although several officers and men were killed or wounded by these deadly marksmen on *July 2*, few visitors realize that the heaviest fighting between sharpshooters occurred on July 3. All day on the third, everything that could be done to drive the Confederates from Devil's Den was tried – but all failed. Finally, late in the day near sunset, a portion of Crawford's Division of the Fifth Corps advancing from the Union right (near the northern base of Little Round Top) made a left wheel and enveloped the Den, dislodging and capturing the Rebs there. Robert Carter of Company H, 22nd Massachusetts Infantry, gives a fine description of the "murderous fellows" who made life so tough for the Federals opposite their position at Devil's Den.

"They came through our lines, and proved to be of the Third Arkansas, Hood's Division, Robertson's Brigade, and were as ragged, unkempt and tough-looking a body of men as it had ever been our fortune to see in the Army of Northern Virginia. They were all dead shots, armed mostly with the old-fashioned muzzle-loading Mississippi, or squirrel rifle, carrying a small pea ball that sounded spitefully murderous, as they sharply sang among the cedars and flattened with a dull, ominous thud against the moss-covered boulders that composed our fortifications."

Captain Cowan's Story

Andrew S. Cowan, captain of the 1st New York Battery, told this battle story of July 3 at the great reunion in 1913.

Cowan said he went into a field hospital to see how his comrades were getting along, and there he found a desperately wounded Confederate. The Rebel was saying to the surgeon, "Doctor, I don't want the news of my being wounded to get out. My wife is about to become a mother, and if she hears of my being shot, it will kill her."

The surgeon managed to keep his name out of the list of wounded.

Twenty-three years later, a young man walked into this same surgeon's office in Plainfield, New Jersey, and said, "Doctor, I have come up here to Princeton (College) and my father told me to come and see you. You saved his life, you saved my mother's life, and you saved my life.

"I am the boy."

The Bloody Hoe Cakes

Edward H. Wade, corporal in Company F, 14th Connecticut Infantry, tells how hungry the men were by the end of the Battle.

"We had scarcely anything to eat from July 1 to the night of the 3rd, when we crawled out on the battlefield after dark, where the enemy's (dead and) wounded lay, and took the haversacks from those who had been killed in the fight that day; these haversacks were nearly all full of nice hoe-cakes. Some that we found were stained with blood where it had run into their haversacks from their wounds. But we were so hungry that we didn't stop for that.

"This may seem a tough story, but it is true."

The Irishman's Song

While attending wounded Confederates near the Codori house along the Emmitsburg Road on the night of July 3, Dan Crotty of the 3rd Michigan Infantry had a melancholy experience.

He writes, "While putting some guns under a poor fellow's head to relieve him, I hear, not far from me, the most plaintive song I ever heard. It put me in mind of my far off home in the Emerald Isle. The strangeness of the scene and manner the song was sung made the tears fall thick and fast down my cheeks.

"Making my way in the direction of the sound, I beheld a sight that chilled the blood in my veins. Before my eyes lay the singer stretched on his back, and eyes looking up at the starry firmament. He did not seem to be in any pain . . . he asked for some water. The 'God bless you' he said more than paid me for all I did that fearful night. He was an Irishman.

"I asked him how he could take up arms against the government that gave him a home. 'Oh,' said he, 'it is all misfortune, and now my dying regret is that I do not die for the starry flag.' I left him in peace."

The Saddest Sight

"One of the saddest sights I ever witnessed was . . . a soldier with a North Carolina regiment mark in his cap leaning against a fly tent. A fragment of a shell had struck him above the breastbone and tore the whole stomach lining away leaving exposed his heart and other organs which were in motion and he seemed alive and conscious.

"I lingered a moment for I had never seen anything so shocking . . . !"

PART V

The Retreat and Aftermath

The Amputated Carbuncle

Private O.M. Osborne of Company F, 118th Pennsylvania Infantry, had been detailed to a field hospital to assist in burying amputated limbs. While carrying an armful of legs for burial, he passed two wounded Michigan soldiers playing cards. Anxious to identify his leg lost in the second day's fight, one of the soldiers requested Osborne to halt and permit him to examine the load, explaining, "My leg can be readily distinguished from the others by a carbuncle on the little toe. It gave me much annoyance when I had the entire use of the missing member, and I would just like to see how the ugly parasite is thriving without me."

The Entrepreneurs

Two enterprising young boys found a way to make some money during the day following the Battle. Daniel A. Skelly and a friend, Gus Bentley, both borrowed ten dollars from their mothers and went to the Hollinger warehouse in Gettysburg where Gus knew tobacco had been hidden when the Rebels captured the town. With the twenty dollars, they "invested in the tobacco. It was in large plugs – Congress tobacco, a well-known brand. We cut it up into ten cent pieces and each of us took a basket full."

When they were turned back at the Union lines near Cemetery Hill, the boys "went back into the town – up High Street to the jail, where we turned into a path leading down to the old Rock Creek 'swimming hole.' We kept to the path down to the spring then turned over towards Culp's Hill, ascending it at one of its steepest points. There were all kinds of debris of the Battle scattered over the hill. The breastworks were formidable-looking. The soldiers helped us over the breastworks and in a short time our baskets were empty and our pockets filled with ten cent pieces. We made a number of trips, selling out each time, and paying back our borrowed capital; we each had more money than we ever had before in our lives."

Rotting Corpses

To give the reader an idea how loathsome a human body can become after several days in a hot climate, picture the scene below.

"On the 4th of July, in readjusting and straightening our lines, the guns of Jones' battalion were put in position on a part of the field which Hill's corps had fought over on the 1st, and upon which the pioneer corps and burying parties had not been able to complete their work. Therefore, the dead bodies of men and horses had lain there putrefying under the summer sun for three days. The sights and smells that assailed us were simply indescribable – corpses swollen to twice their original size, some of them actually burst asunder with the pressure of foul gases and vapors. I recall one feature never before noted, the shocking distension and protrusion of the eyeballs of dead men and dead horses. Several human or unhuman corpses sat upright against a fence with arms extended in the air and faces hideous with something very like a fixed leer, as if taking a fiendish pleasure in showing what we essentially were and might at any moment become.

"The odors were nauseating, and so deadly that in a short time we all sickened and were lying with our mouths close to the ground, most of us vomiting profusely. We protested against the cruelty and folly of keeping men in such a position! We were soon moved away; but for the rest of the day and late into the night the fearful odors I had inhaled remained with me and made me loathe myself as if I was already a rotting corpse."

Only a Torso

One of the Sisters of Charity who came to Gettysburg to assist with the wounded was Mary David from St. Joseph's in Emmitsburg. She was in her early 20s in 1863 but even in her last days, in tones trembling with emotion, she would tell of one poor soldier whose arms and legs had been shot off by a shell.

"I can see him now after all these years," she would say, "only the head and trunk of a man as they brought him in and leaned him up against a corner."

The Colonel and the Chaplain

Reverend George Patterson was chaplain of the 3rd North Carolina Infantry, and prior to Lee's retreat from Gettysburg was sent to find a wounded colonel who had been left to die on a certain part of the field. He took a lantern and went out alone and found him. It had become known that the army had orders to withdraw, and the chaplain told the wounded young man that he would be obliged to leave him and march with his regiment. Whereupon the officer asked Chaplain Patterson to read the burial service over him before he left. The colonel said: "For I know I'm as good as dead." To this request, Patterson gave a cheerful assent, and there on the battlefield, in the darkness, by the light of the lantern, the solemn service was read. Then Patterson bade the dying officer farewell.

The colonel did not die, however, but recovered his health and lived for many years afterward.

In the year 1886, in a western town, the colonel saw the old chaplain and walked up to him and cordially greeted him. The minister, however, did not recognize the colonel and, shading his eyes with his hand, looked at him intently a moment and then shook his head, saying "I don't know you, sir. Who are you?" The former officer replied, "I am Colonel Bennett, of the 14th North Carolina Regiment."

To which Reverend Patterson promptly replied, "Now I *know* you are lying, for I buried him at Gettysburg!"

Dick Price Hangs On

After the Battle, heavy rains commenced. "During this rain the waters of Rock Creek rose so rapidly it flooded the hospital grounds along its banks. The attendants were unable to move all the sick as rapidly as the water endangered them.

The water got so high that R.S. Price (a private in Battery B, 1st New Jersey Artillery) was holding himself up with his elbows on the branch of a dogwood tree. His limbs had been amputated. Looking over to Billy Riley, whose wounds had been dressed, who was also climbing, Price said, 'Billy, they talk about Napoleon climbing the Alps; why shouldn't there be a marker to Dick Price climbing the dogwood?"

Price later died. You can visit his grave in the Soldiers' National Cemetery at Gettysburg. His father stood there in 1888 and cried out, "My boy, my boy, O God why did you take my boy?"

View from a Litter

Robert Stiles, a major in the Confederate artillery tells a story of his friend on the retreat from Gettysburg. He was a Georgia officer named McDaniel who had been seriously wounded and captured. Several friends who had also been captured and were about to be marched off to prison, came by to bid him good-bye, as the Federal surgeons said he must remain behind as he would surely die on the road.

"Very good," said McDaniel, "I'll die then. I am certainly going, and if you don't bring a litter and put me on it and carry me, then I will simply get up and walk till I drop."

Knowing either way was certain death, the surgeons yielded, and McDaniel began what everyone believed was his funeral procession. The journey for the Georgian was fearful, and he grew weaker and weaker. Finally at a halt in a small Pennsylvania town, as the population gathered around to see the Rebel prisoners, it appeared that McDaniel had passed on to his heavenly reward.

His best friend, Colonel Nesbit, stood guard over the litter and was about to examine his friend to see if the end had come, when McDaniel opened his eyes and beckoned feebly for Nesbit to move closer. When Nesbit reached his side, McDaniel took hold of Nesbit's coat, drew him near and in a voice scarcely audible, whispered, *"Nesbit!"*

Colonel Nesbit says he expected a last message, or a tender farewell, but instead, pointing with a trembling finger, McDaniel uttered these words:

"Nesbit, old fellow! Did you ever see such an ungodly pair of ankles as that Dutch woman on that porch has got?"

Of course, such a man could not be killed. Many years later he was elected Governor of Georgia.

The Hogs Ate It Up!

A New Hampshire captain recalled a gruesome incident on July 4, while visiting a wounded friend, Drake, who had lost a leg on July 2.

"The scene about me was one never to be forgotten. Men were mutilated in all conceivable ways and piles of legs and arms told of the work of the surgeons. Many limbs had been buried, but in shallow trenches, and a brook close by, swollen to large proportions by the heavy rain . . . had uncovered many and these were exposed to view.

"Years later in talking with Comrade Drake . . . I asked him what disposition was made of his leg. 'The hogs ate it up,' was his prompt reply. Then he explained that he felt the pain as the flesh was torn from the bones by the hogs, just as plainly as though the leg had not been amputated."

Officers' Dress

During the retreat from Gettysburg, the Confederate army was in a "sad plight as to clothing. Hundreds had no shoes. Thousands were as ragged as they could be − some with the bottoms of the pants in long frazzles; others with their knees out, others out at the elbows, and their hair sticking through holes in their hats. Some of the men patched their clothing, and it was usually done with any material they could get. One man had the seat of his pants patched with bright red, and his knees patched with black. Another had used a piece of gray or brown blanket. There were, however, so few patches and so many holes that, when a Pennsylvania girl on the side of the road saw us pass and asked her mother how the officers were distinguished from the privates, the mother replied that it was easy enough: the officers' pants were patched, and the privates' pants were not."

Another Look at Henry Wentz

One of the old time human interest stories centered around the Battle of Gettysburg, is that of Henry Wentz, a soldier in the Confederate artillery who had, prior to the War, lived just southwest of the town where the famed "Peach Orchard" was and still is located. Supposedly, in the 1850s, he had gone to Virginia to make his living in the carriage-building trade. When the war broke out, he joined a Southern unit and, as circumstances would have it, Henry found himself fighting on his father's property on July 2 and 3. The story reports how he visited his father once or twice during the Battle. It is a wonderful account, and ends nicely enough. However, Lieutenant Jackson of the 16th Michigan Infantry wrote something in his memoirs which may have a different bearing on this story.

"On Sunday morning, July 5th, I was ordered to take a detail of men from my regiment and proceed to that part of the field near the Emmitsburg Road in the direction of the peach orchard, for the purpose of burying the Confederate dead. I took up my work near the (Wentz) house. I ordered the men to dig a trench in the garden to the left and in front of the house, near the road. Later, I looked up and saw an old man and old woman approaching. They were the owners of the house.

"They turned into the yard, but instead of noticing the partial destruction, at least, of their home, barn, out-houses, fences, etc., they busied themselves in gathering the tender branches of the mulberry tree or bush – for what purpose, I could not determine, until they entered the house, which was a 1½ story log building literally perforated by shot and shell, and climbed the stairway to the attic where, suspended from the rafters, were hammocks filled with silkworms, which they commenced to feed. I engaged them in conversation. They told me of their work, etc. In a short time we descended to the front of their house. The bodies of the dead were being hauled in from the field to the trench and among the number was an artillery officer.

"Papers were found upon the body indicating the same name as the family. I called their attention to it. They replied, 'Yes, yes we had a son who left our home and went to Virginia. The last we heard of him he was in Confederate service. But we disowned our son and will have nothing to do with the body if it is he.'

"I buried the remains in the trench with others. Think of this incident for a moment. This disowned son, a Rebel, killed and buried in the door yard where he was brought up – how pathetic."

The Dead Man "Stood Up"

Sergeant Wyman S. White of Company F, 2nd U.S. Sharpshooters Regiment, came across an unusual sight while visiting the area near Devil's Den on July 6.

"At another place we saw a Rebel's body standing up almost straight beside a big rock. His rifle lay over the top of the stone and his arms were extended on top of the rock. From appearance, I should think he was about to fire when he was hit and instantly killed, falling forward onto the stone and as his body swelled, it straightened up so as to be in a standing position."

Incident on the Plank Farm

One of the most heart-rending incidents I have ever read concerning the suffering of wounded men occurred a few days after the Battle in a field hospital located on the Plank farm southwest of Gettysburg.

Private W.C. Ward of Company G, 4th Alabama Infantry, had been wounded on July 2. It was now July 7 and Ward and a companion lay in an apple orchard at the farm, suffering from exposure, hunger, and untreated wounds.

"Great green flies in swarms of millions gathered, grown unnaturally large, fattened on human blood. Fever-smitten, pain-racked, there came to us another terror; we were to be devoured while living by maggots – creeping, doubling, crawling in among the nerves and devouring the soldier while yet alive.

"A comrade from Marion, Alabama, who lay on his back on the ground until great sores had eaten into his body, discovered one day that he was bleeding very rapidly from his wound. A tourniquet was placed – (which) every movement of the body displaced. Whenever he would find himself bleeding, he would call out, 'Quick, quick!' (I) would roll over and place a thumb and finger on the bleeding artery and cry for help.

"For 48 hours this struggle went on. The blood had accumulated in a pool from the point of his hip to his heel and in the blood the maggots were rioting in their gory feast and reveling in the poor fellow's wound. The noise they made as they doubled and twisted, crept and crawled, was that of hogs eating corn. Lying on his stomach (because he could not sit up), the soldier dipped away, by the aid of a spoon with which he (then) fed himself a half gallon of these terrible insects.

"The surgeons at last did something; they ligated the artery, and saved the man.

"The brave fellow still lives and has served his generation well in Marion, Alabama."

The James River Brothers

Lieutenant John R. Presgraves, Company I, 8th Virginia Infantry, who was wounded severely at Gettysburg was lucky indeed, to have a devoted brother to care for him. A nurse, Miss Clarissa F. Jones of Philadelphia, recalled their intense brotherly love.

"I will never forget my first case. He was a young fellow, lying on a rock, and suffering intensely. Beside him was his brother, nursing and caring for him. The anxious brother did not even have a handkerchief; he was bathing the boy's wounds with a piece of paper. I was burdened with handkerchiefs and gave the Rebel a few. I stayed with him some time, bandaged his wounds and his brother told me his story. They lived on the James River. He said he had two other brothers in the Battle, and he feared they had both been killed. When he saw this brother fall, he allowed himself to be taken prisoner, so that he could be with him. He knew his brother was going to die. 'How am I going back to my father and tell him of this. I am afraid that I am the only one left. My poor father! He was more like a big brother to us and you don't know how much we loved him!'

"He was so affectionate to his brother, and waited on him night and day. Four days later the poor young fellow died."

Amazingly, Miss Jones reports that the surviving brother was able to procure a pine coffin for John (a rare find in that area after the Battle) and had him buried properly at the Second Corps Hospital. Miss Jones says that, after burying John, he told her he was going to escape — which he did a few days later. No one ever saw or heard from him again.

Death Be Not Proud

The following scene should take away any notion from visitors to Gettysburg that war is glorious in any way.

"We found a dead soldier lying on his face, his hands clenched, his eyes set, the earth all about him clotted with blood. Immediately in the center of his back, just below the shoulders, was a ghastly wound made by a shell which had carried away a solid mass of flesh, and left exposed the vital parts . . . the agony had become too great to bear, and with none to help, the poor sufferer had died by inches. In his agony, he had clutched and loosened the earth as far as he could reach; and there, with his face fallen into the pit his own hands had made, he lay on the field where he had hoped, perhaps, to win distinction and whence, it may be, he had expected to send news of victory."

A Rebel "Scam"

A near disaster befell a U.S. Sanitary Commission Relief Agent from New York who was in an area just vacated by the Confederates after their retreat from Gettysburg Evidently some deserters or bushwackers remained behind to do mischief after the main part of Lee's army had gone. His diary gives the details:

Saturday, July 11, 1863 — "Started for Waynesboro from Chambersburg at 7:30 a.m. It was a lonely ride, and I came near having an adventure — I met a man on the road who invited me to go to his house to have a 'drink.' I declined for a certain something told me not to go, so pushing on reached Waynesboro at 10 o'clock, my horse completely used up. Joe Leggit came over the road two hours later, met the same man, started for his house with him but thinking it too far to go just for a drink, returned to the main road and was run for two miles by a squad of Johnnies.

"Joe's horse brought him through safe, but I cannot but think where my three-legged brute would have left me."

The Defiant Colonel

After the Battle of Gettysburg, a Christian Commission delegate, moving among the wounded giving sympathy and aid, came to a wounded officer from South Carolina. The delegate said, "Colonel, can I do anything for you?" *"No,"* was the reply, with stubborn defiance. He continued on.

By and by, the delegate came around again, made a similar inquiry, and was again refused. Yet he returned a third time to the officer. The air had become offensive from heat and wounds and he was putting cologne on the handkerchiefs of one and another, as he passed. "Colonel, let me put some of this on your handkerchief," he said. The wounded and suffering man burst into tears, and said "I have no handkerchief." "Well, you shall have one," and wetting his own with cologne, he gave it to him. The colonel was now ready to talk. Said he, "I can't understand you Yankees; you fight us like devils, and then you treat us like angels.

"I am sorry I entered this war."

Their Fifth Son

So many pathetic scenes took place during the Battle and aftermath. Here is one told by a girl of 13, Lydia Catherine Zeigler, who lived with her parents in the Old Dorm at the Lutheran Theological Seminary. In 1900, she recalled:

"Late in the afternoon, about a week after the battle, I remember going into the yard and finding there an old man supporting the head of a sweet faced old lady on his shoulder. I walked up and asked if I could be of any assistance, for I saw the old lady looked faint and weary. The answer came from the trembling lips of the old gentleman: "'Mother's most tuckered out, but if we can find our boy, Charlie, I guess she will be all right.' I listened to their pitiful story of losing four sons in the war, and knowing their last son had been in the Battle of Gettysburg, they walked all the twenty-one miles over the mountain from Chambersburg, carrying a satchel filled with dainties such as Charlie was fond of.

"Charlie was found lying in one of the rooms of the third floor of the Seminary in a dying condition. The cries of that mother as she bent over the body of her boy were heartbreaking. For a short time consciousness returned to Charlie, and he knew his parents, who had at least some measure of comfort in taking his dead body home for burial."

The Sharpshooter's Skeleton

A Union soldier visiting the Battlefield of Gettysburg seventeen days after the fight to locate the grave of his brother, came across another soldier of the Pennsylvania Reserves who had had *his* brother killed by a Rebel sharpshooter, and who showed him the following:

"On the north side of Big Round Top and near the summit, I saw the whitening bones of a Johnny who had killed and wounded 17 of our men during the night. He rolled a rock as big as a bushel basket ahead of him, while he crawled behind it. He could see our men toward the sky, while they could see only the flash of his gun, which they shot at all night. At dawn, he could not retreat and our boys 'got him.' They could not dig a grave there. They cut brush and laid it across him, head down hill, and carried dirt and weighted down the ends of the brush. His head had rolled down hill some 10 feet; his shoes with the bones of his feet had fallen sidewise and lay there. A soldier of the Reserves was there that night and showed me and explained as above."

A "Methodist Nun"

Both the Catholic Church on West High Street and the Methodist Church on East Middle Street were used as hospitals in Gettysburg, and both were fortunate to have a few Sisters of Charity working as nurses therein. These nurses were well-known and easily recognized by the nun's habit they wore.

One day one of the Sisters stationed at the Catholic Church went into the store operated by the Sanitary Commission at the corner of Baltimore Street and Middle Street to order supplies for her hospital. Soon after, a Sister stationed at the Methodist Church called at this store and left her order. As she was leaving, the clerk said: "Where are these articles to be sent? I believe you belong to the Catholic Church."

"No, sir," replied the Sister, "I belong to the Methodist Church. Send the goods there."

The Doctor Finds His Brother

Lieutenant John C. Warren, 52nd North Carolina Infantry, was 18 years old when he was struck by five bullets at Gettysburg. Left to die by Federal surgeons, he lay covered in blood and filth for two weeks. By a unique coincidence, the lieutenant's brother, Dr. L.P. Warren, a brigade surgeon, was one of the medical men left behind by General Lee when the Army of Northern Virginia retreated to Virginia.

One day while treating some of the thousands of Confederate wounded, Dr. Warren discovered his brother, John, by now on the very edge of death. Dr. Warren attended him for several days, thereby saving his life.

Although the lieutenant hovered between life and death for many weeks, he survived, living until 1914.

The Wandering Pig

A private in the 154th New York, writing to his wife from the Eleventh Corps Hospital at Gettysburg, told a good tale on the Confederates.

"Even amongst so much suffering and death, some things laughable will occur.

"The other day we had some wounded Rebs in the cellar of the barn and, the door being open, a stray pig walked in. One of the Rebs entered a complaint to the Doctors' waiting boy that we allowed hogs to roam about among their wounded.

"The boy asked him if the hog recognized any *acquaintances* among the Rebs!"

A "Plucky" Johnnie

The huge field hospital of Hancock's Second Corps was located in the woods on the old Moses Schwartz farm. "And here in this wood, I saw one of the pluckiest Johnnies I ever got eyes on. He must have been fully six feet in height with a pleasant face and a piercing black eye. He was entirely nude for there was no portion of his body from head to foot that would endure the friction of clothing. He could not lie, he could not sit. The only position he could occupy was to rest himself on the tips of his fingers and the tips of his toes and thus move about from place to place, to some extent.

"He was the worst scarred up man I had ever seen. He was wounded every place. You have heard as a figure of speech of a man looking as if he had been through a threshing machine or a stone crusher — yet apparently he did not have a mortal wound.

"The last I saw of him he was moving around, in his snail like way, taking observations of forest scenery. I have no doubt he got well promptly. It would take more than a couple of dozen cuts and bruises to kill anyone with that Johnnie's pluck."

The Wounded Woman Rebel

Many know of the Confederate woman who was found dead on the field of Pickett's Charge and was buried by the men of Hay's Brigade on July 3. However, another female was certainly in the fighting at Gettysburg. In a letter written by a wounded Michigan man from the U.S. Military Hospital in Chester, Pennsylvania, this interesting account emerges.

"I must tell you we have got a female secesh here. She was wounded at Gettysburg, but our doctors soon found her out. I have not seen her, but they say she is very good looking. The poor girl has lost a leg. It is a great pity she did not stay at home with her mother but she gets good care and kind treatment. But it is rather romantic to have a female soldier in the hospital and her only to have one leg and far away from home, but I hope she will soon get better and get home to her friends."

Glowing Graves

What must have been a frightful phenomenon to local residents who had burials on their property was described by Mr. T. Duncan Carson, a bank clerk in Gettysburg.

"On my uncle's farm, just below Big Round Top, hundreds of the dead were buried in a single trench. They were covered very shallow, and at night you could see phosphorescent light coming out of the earth where they were buried."

A Confederate assistant surgeon described this unusual light in a more detailed way.

"As I approached I saw each grave marked out in its whole extent by a ghastly phosphorescent gleam floating over it. I got off my horse and made as critical examination as I could. The light did not develop till the exhalation had risen some two feet above the grave. It was of a pronounced blue color, which, though pallid in its tint, was very distinct and conspicuously visible, and of uniform tenuity without glow or coruscation. It was very sensitive to air currents, and I could make it vanish by a wave of my hand, but in a few seconds it would glide into sight again after a very ghostly fashion . . . . Some few nights after this apparition I passed the haunted spot again, but the jack-o-lanterns were gone."

The "Dutch" Farmer

While most of the people of Gettysburg made a good reputation by doing everything they could for the 22,000 wounded left after the Battle, unfortunately many Adams County farmers gained a reputation for being cruel, uncaring, tight-fisted, and utterly disinterested in the suffering of these men. One story illustrates what the soldiers thought of this type of individual.

"If at any time you would like to swear, call your enemy a 'Dutch farmer' – nothing can be worse. The Dutch farmers of Gettysburg have made themselves a name and a fame to the latest day, by charging our poor men, who crawled out of the barns and woods where they hid themselves after they were wounded, 3 or 4 dollars each for bringing all that was left of their poor bodies, after defending the contemptible Dutch firesides, down to the railroad.

"The day before we came away, a sleeping-looking stupid Dutchman walked into camp, having heard we had 'some Rebels.' He lived 5 miles from (Gettysburg) and had 'never seen one,' and came mooning in to stare at them, and stood with his mouth open. 'And why didn't you take your gun and help drive them out of your town?' Mother said. *'Why, a feller might a got hit;'* at which the Rebels lying in double rows in the tent, shook themselves almost to pieces."

Human Specimens

One particular note on the aftermath of the Battle is the fact that many soldiers' bodies were being taken and prepared as medical specimens. Dr. Theodore Dimon, a medical relief agent from New York, recalled "a man of science gathering specimens of broken bones." A resident of Gettysburg, Mr. J.E. Jacobs, after a tour of the Battlefield, reported "medical students preparing skeletons, and in a cauldron, boiling the remains of heroes."

Hard to believe, but true; just another in the thousands of incidents connected with the great Battle.

Risqué Business

It may seem remarkable to most people that the following situation could have developed so close to the thousands of wounded and dying men. It was reported by J. Howard Wert, a local man who spent months in and among the field hospitals around Gettysburg.

"Amongst the early arrivals were three women. They were not very prepossessing to look at for they carried with them foxy faces, weasel-like eyes and a heart-hiding smile that chilled like dagger points . . . their names were Mrs. Smith, Mrs. Jones, and Mrs. Brown, so they said. They were promptly supplied with a wall tent, and this they pitched contiguous to one of the barns used as a hospital. They were supplied with an ambulance, and accompanied by a hospital attendant dressed in blue, (as they) solicited butter, eggs, poultry and aught else that was choice. They told harrowing tales of the distress of the poor wounded boys and received liberal contributions.

"Each night after the trip amongst the farms and villages, a symposium was held in the wall tent adjacent to the barn. High jinks were celebrated till well on into the wee hours. (They were) assisted by certain able-bodied soldiers who had been left back by the army as hospital officials and attendants. Brandy and wine, the seals on which showed brands the rarest, came in copious quantities from the cellars of Baltimore and Philadelphia. A generous share of this, too, found its way to the wall tent.

"Each night the revel grew louder and louder and finally it grew too loud – as proprieties were flung to the winds in the wall tent."

"Before long, however, a conscientious surgeon told the provost marshal, and the jig was up. Mrs. Smith, Jones, and Brown left Adams County very suddenly under humiliating circumstances, as did several hospital attendants who found themselves in the combatant ranks of the Army of the Potomac which was now near Mine Run, Virginia."

The President's Nephew

"We had a nephew of Jefferson Davis, President of the Confederate States of America, in our camp. Poor fellow, he suffered terribly. A special chair was rigged up for him because his back was injured, but he begged so hard to be taken out of it that the doctors consented. No matter in what position he was placed, he was not satisfied. When the orders came to take the men to Camp Letterman, the Union men had considerable trouble in lifting him into the wagon, he suffered so. Finally, one gruff soldier said, 'That's what you get for fighting against us.' But the poor fellow answered in a kindly voice, 'I fought against you only once, and I'll never fight again. And remember, my dear man, the Lord says that you must forgive if they fight seventy times seven."

Escape from Letterman

Most of the Confederate soldiers captured in the Gettysburg Battle were quickly moved away from the Union army's rear area to Westminster, Maryland, and from there to military prisons in Maryland, Delaware, Ohio, New York and Illinois. However, we often forget that all Confederate wounded were, in fact, prisoners of war, and were left behind only until they were well enough to travel. Several thousands were in the field hospitals at Gettysburg, and a few lingered here until November.

During the months from July to November, a few Rebels were able to escape either alone or with the help of Southern sympathizers. The provost guards at the hospitals were constantly on the lookout for male and female visitors attempting to smuggle in civilian clothing which would enable Confederates to more easily escape detection until they were safely south of the Mason-Dixon line. One enterprising Reb, however, *was* able to make a "break" and his story is worth repeating. He was Sergeant Charles Jones Beck, of a South Carolina regiment and he was wounded on July 2 and first taken to the hospital at the Black Horse Tavern. Later he was "captured" by the Federals and sent to Camp Letterman, the U.S. General Hospital near Gettysburg. In 1901, he wrote:

"I plotted my escape from this hospital with Thomas C. Paysinger, Company E, 3rd

South Carolina Regiment, on or about the first of September. We went into dinner but pretended not to care for anything to eat and then left the mess. We approached a sentinel near the camp graveyard and asked permission to visit the grave of an alleged brother of Paysinger whom we told the sentinel had just died. The sentinel gave the permission and as soon as his back was turned, we jumped the fence into the woods and made the escape. On our way homeward through Maryland, we stopped at a house where we were very kindly treated by the ladies, to whom we gave our names and they in turn did the same. They requested that we notify them if we arrived home safely. At Richmond, Virginia, we separated; I, making my way back to Columbia, South Carolina.

"The ladies were burned out by the Yankees in 1865 and we have made repeated efforts to find them. They lived on the Monocacy River, about a mile from the Potomac.

"I should be glad to hear from them again . . . !"

The Sleeping Reb

Camp Letterman was located one mile east of Gettysburg on the York Pike. It was a huge general hospital set up in order to more efficiently handle the thousands of wounded left behind after the Battle. (It is now, sadly, a shopping center and trailer park.)

In a letter home to his brother on October 26, 1863, Frank Stoke recalls an unusual incident which happened there.

"One morning while I was on guard between the hospital and the graveyard, the Ward-master and two nurses passed me with a Confederate soldier, taking him to the dead-house. After they had passed me a few steps, the supposed dead man partly raised himself up on the stretcher and asked what they intended to do with him. They all took a hearty laugh and turned around and carried him back to camp!

"For all I know he is living yet."

The Deadly Photograph

The history of Camp Letterman, the huge general hospital east of Gettysburg, extended from late July to about December 1, when it was finally totally disbanded. Its history is filled with color, tragedy, humor, suffering, and pathos.

One unfortunate event happened there to a soldier named Peter Brock. To illustrate the callousness of *some* surgeons, it is worth repeating. A nurse at the Camp, Miss Bucklin, says:

"One fine-looking fellow, a son of Erin's Isle, was provoked by the neglect, and declared, with emphasis, that he would have his wounded shoulder examined by a surgeon. He finally succeeded, by perseverance, in obtaining an examination.

"He was found to be in a very critical situation, and one after another of the surgeons were called in, till a regular council of doctors was held over him. It was found necessary to take off a section of the bone, and the operation was begun in full view of the other patients.

"After mangling him there for a time, partly holding him under the influence of chloroform, they removed him to the amputating room, where they paused awhile to have their photographs taken, the suffering patient lying in this critical condition. My blood boiled at the cruelty of the scene. For three hours he was kept under the knife and saw, and I was directed to hold my peace. He was brought back to his bed, as white as a dead man in his coffin . . . !"

"I Don't See It, Boys!"

In an earlier story, a Rebel who was being carried to the dead-tent at the General Hospital to await burial, rose up and startled those around him. In this, a similar tale, Luther White, Company K, 20th Massachusetts Infantry from Boston, pulls the same "trick."

Private White had been wounded by a piece of shell, which tore off part of his ear and, shattering his jaw, exposed one side of his throat. After the Battle, he remained unconscious for three days, then rallied; and again sank away until he died – as it was thought, and was being carried to his grave.

"The stretcher bearers came tramping wearily, bearing three bodies. As the last reached the graveyard at the Second Corps Hospital, the men dropped the army couch whereon he rested. The impatient effort to be rid of their burden was probably the means of saving a life; for the man – *dead* as they supposed – raising his head, called in a clear voice: 'Boys, what are you doing?' The response was prompt: 'We came to bury you, Whitey.' His calm reply was: 'I don't see it, boys; give me a drink of water and carry me back.' And then glancing into the open grave: 'I won't be buried by this raw recruit!' The raw recruit was a lieutenant of his own regiment!

"Not many stand so near the 'dark valley' that they look into their own graves and *live.* "

One Woman's Devotion

A wife came to see and care for her wounded husband of the 13th Massachusetts. Learning he was dead, she asked about his grave and was told, "You might as well expect to find a needle in a haystack." "Then," she replied, "I can find him; for I could take apart every blade of hay until I had removed it entirely. Show me where he was buried."

After disinterring nearly twenty bodies, the woman saw a particular button on the corpse in the next grave by which she knew her husband. This button on his uniform had been dented by a bullet in a previous battle, and the woman remembered it well. Jumping into the hole, she scratched the dirt off of his body. After removing him from this un-marked resting place, the devoted wife accompanied her soldier to their Northern home.

The Perfect Stump

One soldier became quite a celebrity due to the loss of part of his leg at Gettysburg. Here is his letter.

Chestnut Hill Hospital
Philadelphia - September 20, 1863

Surgeon Ebersole

As your amputation of my limb at the knee-joint causes much curiosity among the surgeons here, I thought I would let you know about it. They say it is one of the best amputations they ever saw. (One) said it was the prettiest stump that he ever saw. You do not know how I was annoyed the first five days by the surgeons here coming to see my stump.

The surgeon in charge told the doctor of this ward to have a picture taken of my stump. So, if they take it, I will have one sent to you. I was at Palmer's office yesterday, and measured for a new leg. Palmer says I have such a nice stump for an artificial leg. I will close with thanks to you for your skill in taking off my limb.

From your humble Servant
Sergeant Alexander Ivey
Co. D, 7th Wisconsin Volunteers

An Honest Officer

One of the most fascinating reasons ever given by an officer in tending his resignation, was that of Second Lieutenant Donald Gillies, 125th New York Infantry.

His dismissal from the service was confirmed "on the grounds that a wound received in the Battle of Gettysburg has so intimidated him that he has become constitutionally a coward and unfit to lead his company into action."

Close Calls

With a total of over 7,000 killed in the three days of battle, and over 20,000 wounded, imagine how many close calls occurred. Here is a small sample:

Private T.J. Wrangham, of Company C, 123rd New York Infantry, was crossing the breastworks on Culp's Hill when a bullet struck the "U.S." brass plate on his cartridge box, passed through that and the thick leather flap, then through the tin box which held the cartridges, and lodged in the leather next to his hip.

Lieutenant Isaac Plumb, 61st New York Infantry, was struck by a bullet and knocked down near the Wheatfield on July 2. He supposed that the bullet had gone through him and he was done for. He clapped his hand over the "wound" but found that no blood was apparent. Later he discovered that the bullet had struck his sword belt plate squarely and had glanced so as to go under the plate and into his vest pocket where it met a bunch of keys on a ring. The force had embedded the bullet into the keys and ring, but had done no damage to the officer.

Private Tom Gardner, Company H, 14th Connecticut Infantry, had a bullet plow a permanent furrow along the top of his head on July 3.

Sergeant Gregg of Company A, 3rd Pennsylvania Cavalry, had the top of his scalp sliced off by a Confederate saber in the fight against Stuart on July 3. He had only to remove his hat to show a head as neatly tonsured as a monk's.

Private Frederick Frey, Company F, 108th New York Infantry, had the tip of his nose shot off and his rifle shot from his hands during the Battle.

John Shifely of Company D, Pennsylvania Reserves, was saved by his Bible, through which a ball passed without injuring him.

Mrs. Nellie E. Leeds and her husband, living on Carlisle Street in Gettysburg, were talking to a Union soldier on July 1 when a sharpshooter fired at the soldier. The bullet struck a button on his blouse and glanced off. He calmly removed the dented button and handed it to her saying, "Young ladies are generally fond of souvenirs; maybe you would like to have this one."

Although the foregoing were all incidents of "average" men having close calls, many ranking officers, including *Generals,* came very near death at Gettysburg. In fact, General George G. Meade, commander of the Army of the Potomac, had at least five narrow misses between July 2 and July 3!

Adams County Civilians

In several of the stories reported in this booklet, there are references to the behavior of certain farmers in the Gettysburg area. Were they as bad as has been noted in these accounts? The following may be of interest.

One of the best diaries that has been preserved from the Civil War is that of Charles Wainwright, an artillery officer with the Army of the Potomac. In one sentence he summed up his feelings toward Adams County when he stated, "the citizens have damned themselves with a disgrace that can never be washed out."

He and many other Union soldiers were disappointed with the conduct of some civilians in the Gettysburg area. One officer reported that he knew of 300-500 "Copperheads" in

Adams County. "Copperhead" was the name given to Northern people in sympathy with the Confederates. General Patrick, Provost Marshal of the Army of the Potomac, said in his diary that "the people here nearly all are copperheads." And as one Federal soldier remembered, he had to pay a Pennsylvania blacksmith for some small service, "whose fireside and home I was hastening to defend," and he found it startling that such greed and selfishness were so blatantly displayed. Another wrote: "My opinion is that this area of Pennsylvania is *not* Union; thousands have visited the field and I did not see one act of charity."

It *is* a fact that hungry Northern soldiers were refused food, or charged exorbitant prices, such as 75¢ to $1.00 for a loaf of bread which usually sold for 10¢. Several farmers even removed the pump handles from their wells to keep wounded or thirsty men from obtaining a drink of water. Many wounded men recalled how they were charged $1.00 to $4.00 a head by "Dutch" farmers to transport them to field hospitals or to the railroad depot when they were unable to walk.

On the other hand, *most* of both Union and Confederate accounts of contact with *Gettysburg* citizens show a tremendous spirit of generosity and kindness, especially to the wounded. It has become apparent in my research that there was a clear distinction between the "typical" Adams County farmer and the Gettysburg *town* resident.

One, the country "Dutch" farmer, was called an "evil beast," "low type, and mean, and sordid," while the village resident was portrayed to be just the opposite. However, I would like to be very clear on this. This section is not intended to be a generalization, because it just is not fair to do so. My point is to show another side of the war in this area, not often read about. There were many good citizens in the county; in fact, one, a Mr. H.A. Picking was so kind to the wounded Rebels in his home, that at harvest time they worked in his fields, willingly, to bring in his crops. But meanness did exist, as is illustrated in the following story told by Robert S. Robertson of the 93rd New York Infantry.

"One farmer presented to the Quartermaster a bill for 37½ cents for a few bricks knocked off his chimney by a shell. For a joke, he was referred from one officer to another without success, until at last he got to General O.O. Howard, who had lost an arm in service at Fair Oaks in 1862. The General, tapping his empty sleeve and referring to the 37½ cents said, 'My friend, give it to your country, as I did this.'

"The old man left, quite dissatisfied, and the last I heard, he was still looking for the right man to pay the bill."

PART VI

Post War

These Honored Dead?

The Soldiers' National Cemetery at Gettysburg is one of the most important places to visit while viewing the Battlefield. It is the final resting place of many of the Federal soldiers killed in the Battle. Only Union dead were, of course, allowed to be interred there and Lincoln humbly and beautifully consecrated the ground when he delivered his famous address near there in November of 1863. But are all of the dead in the National Cemetery actually Union men?

It may be interesting to know that at least three graves have been identified so far which contain, *not* the supposed sacred bodies of Northern heroes, but the bones of Rebels; enemies of the very men they lie beside!

One of these Confederates is buried in the Massachusetts section under the name of J.L. Johnson, Company K, 11th Massachusetts Infantry. Johnson was actually a member of the 11th Mississippi and was somehow incorrectly identified and ended up in a Yankee grave.

How many more Southerners rest here, uneasily, so far from home?

Miss "Tommy" Kamoo

It is an unfortunate fact that women's participation in the Battle of Gettysburg, as well as the Civil War, has mostly been overlooked. Too often, stories involving women in the ranks are not documented well enough to positively identify either the person or her actions. The following is such a case.

In 1904, a Lancaster, Pennsylvania, newspaper reported that Mrs. Abrev Kamoo had recently died in a Boston hospital. According to the article, Kamoo had been born in Tunis in 1815, and had later attended the University of Heidelberg. In 1862 she had come to the U.S. where she disguised herself as "Tommy" Kamoo and immediately joined the Union Army. During the War she served as a nurse and drummer, her sex being kept hidden all the while. Mrs. Kamoo said she took part in the Battle of Gettysburg where she was slightly wounded in the nose.

Deadly Explosives after Many Years

A popular human interest story associated with this Battle is that of Mary Virginia Wade, and how she became the only civilian to be killed in the greatest battle in American history. This book has also mentioned two other civilians who were wounded during combat on July 1 – John Burns and J.W. Weakley. These next facts may be of interest concerning additional "citizen" casualties.

Three other non-combatants were wounded during the fighting. They were Jacob Gilbert, a Mr. McIlhenny, and Amos M. Whetstone. Gilbert was a long-time resident of the town and was struck in the upper left arm while walking on Middle Street. Whetstone, a Seminary student was hit in the leg by a sharpshooter on Chambersburg Street. Two of these wounds occurred on July 4, during the Confederate retreat.

Charles M. McCurdy wrote a memoir in 1929 and remembered that two of his chums were killed several months after the Battle while trying to open unexploded artillery shells. Albert McCreary in 1909 recalls, "A schoolmate of mine found a shell, he struck it upon a rock and made a spark which exploded the shell. We carried him to his home, and the surgeons did what they could, but he died in about an hour.

"The only other accident that I witnessed happened a year after the Battle. I was passing along High Street, and had reached Power's stoneyard, when I heard a terrible explosion behind me. I saw a young schoolmate lying on his back with his bowels blown away. Near him was a man almost torn to pieces, his hands hanging in shreds."

Another accident was recorded in September 1863. "Mr. Michael Crilly was engaged in an effort to unload a shell, it exploded and seriously injured his hand, requiring the amputation of three fingers."

In March of 1864, "several boys, aged about 15 years, were amusing themselves with a gun from the battlefield, when the contents discharged and entered the head of a little colored girl, inflicting a mortal wound. She died on Wednesday aged about 7 years."

And later that year in June, "Mr. Adam Taney, Jr., residing in Fairfield, met with a serious accident while attempting to open a shell found in one of the fields. The shell exploded and some of the fragments struck him in the feet which may cripple him for life."

Imagine how many more of these incidents went unreported – months, and even years after the fighting, all as a direct result of the Battle of Gettysburg.

A Ghost Story

Whenever a Confederate died at the field hospital located on the Cunningham farm, the owner buried him in a corner of his orchard. Soon there were two long rows of these graves. After the war, these burial places were carefully tended by Mr. Cunningham.

During these same years, Mr. Cunningham employed a Negro boy on the farm by the name of Anthony Jackson. Jackson's brother, Billy, lived at another farm just over the hill where the orchard stood. The two boys were always eager to be together after the day's work was done, but neither would cross the hill alone after dark for fear of the Rebel soldiers buried there. Both swore they could hear chains rattling up there!

Mr. Cunningham assured them repeatedly that these men had *no* chains when they were buried.

But both boys always answered: "Well, we don' nos where dem dead men gots 'em, but they sho gots 'em now!"

An Operation Performed 21 Years Later

In 1884, twenty-one years after the Battle, this little article appeared in a veteran's newspaper.

"A bullet, with which Henry Southern of Greenville, South Carolina, was wounded in the neck at the Battle of Gettysburg, has just been taken from beneath his collarbone by a surgeon. The bullet was not disfigured, and looked as new as it was when it entered his neck."

A Fifty-Year-Old "Find"

"Andrew Wall and I were two of the 6,000 veterans in gray that went to the Gettysburg Encampment.

"On Wednesday about seven or eight of us, blue and gray together, took a tramp over the battlefield. We went down Confederate Avenue to the Spangler House, where we refreshed ourselves with cool water and lemonade, and then continued our march. We went to Devil's Den then to Little Round Top. The walk was about 10 miles, and I enjoyed it in spite of my 72 years.

"On the morning of July 2 out on one of the avenues, I was talking to a comrade, who said: 'Here is where my command was during the fight, and right here the spear was shot off the top of our flagstaff. I am going to look in the weeds and leaves and see if I can find it.' He began to poke about in the dirt, and suddenly he grabbed at something and held it tight against his breast.

"He had really found the spear (tip) after it had lain there fifty years!"

Lost at Gettysburg

George Dietz, a one-time resident of Chester, Pennsylvania, and a Civil War veteran had a most unusual experience in October of 1899. Dietz, who became a Honolulu jeweler, had lost a watch during the fighting at Gettysburg, thirty-six years earlier.

Harry Ellis, a Spanish-American War Volunteer from Kansas, was docked in the Hawaiian Islands for a short time, on his way to Manila on a military transport.

While ashore, Ellis went into Dietz's jewelry store and offered a watch for sale. On being asked where he got it, he said his father, who had found it on the field of Gettysburg, had given it to him. The jeweler, George Dietz, opened it and found his *own name* scratched inside! He lost no time in making a trade with the soldier.

He Visited His Own Grave

There was a man who made a pilgrimage every year to decorate his own grave. He was Stephen Kelly, formerly a member of Company E, 91st Pennsylvania Infantry. He had been discharged in 1864 at the expiration of this three-year term of service.

"Naturally, Kelly was quite shocked some years later when attending the Grand Army of the Republic encampment at Gettysburg, to find his own grave in the National Cemetery. He felt quite hale and hearty and was sure he wasn't dead, but the records said he was. Said he, 'At first the thought shocked me somewhat, but I am used to it now and don't mind it. So, each Decoration Day I go up there and strew some flowers on the tomb of the man who is substituting for me."

They Met Again 50 Years Later

During the 50th Anniversary of the Battle of Gettysburg, a number of old men, some in Confederate grey, others in blue, congregated near the Angle on Cemetery Ridge, the focal point of Longstreet's Assault. It was July 3, 1913, and the average age of these ex-soldiers was 74 years.

A Union veteran overheard a former Rebel explaining: "The place is right here; I was shot right here where I stand now. I would have died if it hadn't been for a Union soldier who saved my life."

The old Federal turned around and remarked, "That's a funny coincidence, I was at the Angle too and there was a Rebel there who was pretty badly hurt. I first gave him a drink of water, and then I took him upon my back and carried him out of the line of fire to the field hospital."

"But, my God," cried the Confederate, "that's just what that Yankee did for me. There couldn't have been two cases just like that at the same time. Let me look at you."

He grabbed the Yankee and looked at him long and earnestly. "You are the man," he said. Further inquiry put it beyond doubt. The Confederate was A.C. Smith of the 56th Virginia and the Union man was Albert N. Hamilton of the 72nd Pennsylvania.

After a comparison of notes, it was made certain that Hamilton had saved Smith as he sank under the Union fire at the Angle, fifty years before.

The Long Lost Sword Hilt

Very near three o'clock on the afternoon on July 3, and just east of Gettysburg on the Rummel farm, Northern cavalry under General David M. Gregg were engaged in mortal hand-to-hand combat with their Southern counterparts who were commanded by General J.E.B. Stuart. In the midst of this confused, clashing mass of men was Captain William E. Miller, a young officer of the 3rd Pennsylvania Cavalry. In this fight, Miller received a blow from a Confederate swordsman which broke his saber blade off near the hilt. Throwing down the now useless weapon, Miller was able to ride to safety.

Over fourteen years later, Captain Miller was with a veterans' party visiting the Rummel farm where the famous cavalry fight had taken place. Looking through a pile of old mixed farm junk and relics collected from the fields by the farmer, Miller noticed a tarnished and rusted saber with most of the blade broken off and gone. Curiosity prompted him to look closer. As he did, William Miller beheld the very weapon he had lost in combat so many years before!

The Story of a Bullet

The following account is the *only story* in this book which did not occur during the Gettysburg Campaign. But it is fantastic, and is one of my all-time favorites.

Private Henry Matthews was a good soldier during the war, and was at the front in some of the hottest engagements of that great struggle. On May 26, 1864, as a member of Company H, 48th Pennsylvania Infantry, he was struck down by a bullet, which entered the back part of his head. The ball passed through a portion of the brain, and was taken out above the forehead. The operation was performed by Dr. W.R.D. Blackwood, the chief division surgeon. During the progress of the operation a mass of the brain, weighing about an ounce and a half and as large as an egg, escaped. The bullet, to which some of the brain matter and a portion of the scalp adhered, was preserved, and when Matthews left the hospital, it was given to him, who, to the astonishment of the surgeon, recovered.

Private Matthews suffered no mental inconvenience, and went on to occupy a responsible clerical position for many years in the Reading Railroad office in Pottsville, Pennsylvania.

When the bullet was presented to him in 1864 at the hospital door, the brain matter and the little patch of scalp had dried up, leaving a few short hairs sticking out from the mass. The bullet had been flattened and somewhat resembled a miniature clam shell in shape.

As time elapsed, Mr. Matthews, who greatly prized this relic, noticed an astonishing fact. The hairs, which at first were scarcely prominent enough to notice, were growing. Other hairs grew out also until a thick black bunch appeared at the back end of the bullet. At first his friends refused to credit the story, although he showed the precious relic in proof. Once or twice, he cut off the ends of the growing hair, and it continued to grow.

In 1883, Matthews went to Philadelphia and sought out Dr. Blackwood, to whom he exhibited the bullet with its bunch of apparently healthy hair. The surgeon, in the presence of professional witnesses, cut off an inch of the hair, measured that which remained, boxed and sealed up the bullet, and placed it in trusty hands for safekeeping.

In 1884, the package was opened. A careful measurement showed that the hair had grown over an inch since the ball had been seen last.

Dr. Blackwood said, "The fact is beyond dispute. Apparently without nutrition, upon the dried up particle of scalp and brain, this hair had been and is now growing, as surely, if not so luxuriantly, as it grew upon Matthews' head when he was shot. I recall the wound, the operation and the presentation of the relic to the injured man after his remarkable recovery."

One More, Just For Fun . . .

On being asked if he had lost his leg in the late war, the stranger, leaning up against the wall of the depot, replied:

"No, I didn't lose that leg in the war. I *used* to claim that my leg was shot off at the Battle of Gettysburg, but one day something happened to cure me of lying.

"I was stumping along the highway in Ohio, and stopped at a farmhouse to beg for dinner.

"'Where did you lose that leg?' asked the woman at the house.

"'At Gettysburg,' I replied.

"'Sit down till I call my husband.'

"He came in from the barn and I was asked where my regiment was stationed during the Battle.

"'In the cemetery,' I replied.

"'Oh! Well, my son Bill was in the cemetery too; I'll call him in.'

"Bill soon came in and he wanted to know what particular gravestone I took shelter behind. I said it was a Scotch granite monument.

"'Oh,' grunted Bill, 'my brother, Bob, was behind just such a stone; I'll call him in.'

"Bob came in and he swore a mighty oath that he was there alone. He knew the monument to a flaw, and remembered the inscription to a word. However, to give me the benefit of the doubt, I was asked my company and regiment.

"'Company B, 35th Ohio,' I answered.

"'Ah, brother Jim was in that regiment, I'll call him in.'

"Jim came in, took a square look at me, and remarked:

"'Stranger, our regiment wasn't within two hundred miles of Gettysburg during all the war!'

"'I said 25th. Of course the 35th wasn't there.'

"'All right, I'll call my brother, Aaron; he was in the 25th.'

"Aaron came in, called me a wooden-legged liar, and I was pitched over the fence into the road.

"They have got this war business down so fine that you can't go around playing tricks in the country anymore. The best way is to own up that you got drunk and got in the way of a locomotive."

THE END

"He would have a sluggish imagination indeed who could stand in the Peach Orchard, the Wheat Field, or Devil's Den, or on Little Round Top, or at the Angle without an overwhelming realization of the will, the agony, and the lives that were spent in trying to seize and to defend them. Here tilled land and pasturage and woodland were suddenly so precious that no amount of blood shed to purchase them was too high a price."

Bernard DeVoto
Harper's Magazine
August, 1937

PART VII
The Sources

PART I

1. A FATEFUL PAIR OF SHOES
   Gleason, D.H.L. A History of the 1st Massachusetts Cavalry. Boston: Houghton, Mifflin & Company, 1891.
2. THE BOOKWORM
   The Gettysburg Compiler, April 24, 1907.
3. THE KNAPSACK
   "Yankee Rebel" - Civil War Journal of Edmund DeWitt Patterson. Chapel Hill: University of North Carolina Press 1966.
4. A PASS TO HEAVEN
   Douglass, Henry K. I Rode with Stonewall. Chapel Hill: University of North Carolina Press, 1940.
5. STOP THE WAR
   Confederate Veteran, February, 1898.
6. THE BARE-BOTTOMED "BUSHWACK"
   Confederate Veteran, September, 1903.
7. HOW DEVIL'S DEN WAS NAMED
   Myers, Elizabeth S. Article in Chattanooga News, October 30, 1913.

PART II

8. MR. WHISTLER'S EARLY MORNING SCARE
   Article in Gettysburg Star and Sentinel. Gettysburg National Military Park Library.
9. THE FIFTH ALABAMA AND THE FIRST DAY
   The War Reminiscences of W.F. Fulton II. Butternut Press Reprint, 1984.
10. THE NAMELESS HEROINE
    Smith, A.P. History of the 76th New York Regiment. Courtland, New York: 1867.
11. JOHN BURNS' WOUNDS
    Jones, H.G. To the Christian Soldiers and Sailors of the Union. Philadelphia: Lippincott's Press, 1868.
12. THE 15 YEAR-OLD "JOHN BURNS"
    The Grand Army Scout and Soldier's Mail, Vol. 5, No. 49, November, 1886.
    The Chronicle. Brookline, Massachusetts, February 16, 1878.
    Cook, B.F. History of the 12th Massachusetts Regiment. Boston: 1882.
13. THE MISSISSIPPIAN
    Journal of the Military Service Institution. June, 1911.
14. SERGEANT STEARNS LOOKS BACK
    Kent, A.A., ed. Three Years with Company K. Fairleigh Dickinson University Press, 1976.
15. THE STEEL VEST
    Journal of the Military Service Institution. June, 1911.
16. BROTHER CAPTURES BROTHER
    New York at Gettysburg. Vol. I. Albany: J.B. Lyon Company, 1900.
17. A HEROIC BUT SELFISH GESTURE
    Bassler, J.H., Reminiscence of the First Day's Fight at Gettysburg. Unpublished address, June, 1895.
18. AN EXCITING ESCAPE
    Butts, J.T., ed. A Gallant Captain of the Civil War. New York: 1902.
19. THE MYSTERIOUS PREDICTION
    Copy of a letter at the University of North Carolina Library.
20. A FISH STORY
    Philadelphia North American, June 29, 1913.
21. A "NERVY" CONFEDERATE
    National Tribune, May, 1900.
22. CHAPLAIN HOWELL'S DEMISE
    Bates, S.P. Pennsylvania Volunteers. Vol. III. Harrisburg: 1869.
    Reflections on the Battle of Gettysburg. Lebanon County Historical Society, Vol. 13, 1963.
    McAllister, Mary. Article in The Philadelphia Inquirer, June, 1938.
    Osborn, William. Letter in The Philadelphia Public Ledger, March, 1911.
    Wills, J.C. Manuscript, Gettysburg National Military Park Library, 1941.
    D.C. Chronicle, July 9, 1863.
23. THE FEDERAL SOLDIER AND ROBERT E. LEE
    Confederate Veteran, Vol. 20, 1912.
24. THE DRINK
    Dickert, D.A. History of Kershaw's Brigade. Dayton, Ohio: Morningside Reprint, 1973.
25. THE ROLLING CHAPLAIN
    Jones, H.G. To the Christian Soldiers and Sailors of the Union. Philadelphia: Lippincott's Press, 1868.
26. STILL A MYSTERY
    Powers, Alice. "Dark Days of Battle Week." The Gettysburg Compiler, July 1, 1903.

PART III

27. HAMPTON'S DUEL
    Mackey, T.J. Article in The Constitution. Atlanta, Georgia: June, 1894.
28. THE APATHETIC CIVILIANS
    Diary of Henry Berkeley, Virginia Historical Society.

66. A MORBID JOKE
"Just The Plain, Unvarnished Story of a Soldier in the Ranks." The New York Times, June 29, 1913.
67. A WOUNDED HORSE
Bowen, J.L. History of the 37th Massachusetts Regiment. C.W. Bryan & Company: 1884.
68. THE FURROW
Copy of letter in author's collection.
69. TO ERR IS HUMAN
"Human Interest Stories" file, Gettysburg National Military Park Library.
70. SLOCUM'S RAGE
Grand Army Scout and Sentinel, Vol. II, No. 22.
71. HIS SON FELL
Official Records of the Union and Confederate Armies. Vol. 27. Washington, D.C.: U.S. Government Printing Of
1898.
72. WHERE IS THE COLORS?
Gettysburg National Military Park Library Files.
73. THE LAST WORDS OF SUMNER PAINE
Harvard Memorial Biographies. Vol. II. Cambridge: Sever and Francis, 1866.
74. A PENNSYLVANIA CIVILIAN IN PICKETT'S CHARGE
Confederate Veteran, Vol. 19, 1911.
75. A DEDICATED COLOR SERGEANT
Copy of letter in author's collection.
76. A SHOCKING DISCOVERY
Journal of the Military Service Institution. June, 1911.
77. MUSKETRY FIRE
Bacon, G.W. and E.W. Howland. Letters of a Family During the War for the Union, 1861-1865. Vol. II. 1899.
78. ARKANSAS SHARPSHOOTERS
Carter, Robert G. Four Brothers In Blue. Austin: University of Texas, 1978.
79. CAPTAIN COWAN'S STORY
The New York Times article, July 3, 1913.
80. THE BLOODY HOE CAKES
Page, Charles D. History of the 14th Connecticut Regiment. Meriden, 1906.
81. THE IRISHMAN'S SONG
Crotty, D.G. Four Years Campaigning with the Army of the Potomac. Grand Rapids, Michigan: 1874.
82. THE SADDEST SIGHT
Houghton, W.R. and T.M.B. Houghton. Two Boys in the Civil War and After. Montgomery, Alabama: Paragon P
1912.

PART V

83. THE AMPUTATED CARBUNCLE
Smith, J.L. History of the 118th Pennsylvania "Corn Exchange" Regiment. Philadelphia: 1905.
84. THE ENTREPRENEURS
Skelly, David A. A Boy's Experience During the Battle of Gettysburg. Gettysburg, Pennsylvania: 1932.
85. ROTTING CORPSES
Stiles, Robert. Four Years Under Marse Robert. Dayton, Ohio: Morningside Reprint, 1977.
86. ONLY A TORSO
Deceased Sisters. Notes on Sister Mary David Solomon, 1932.
87. THE COLONEL AND THE CHAPLAIN
McKim, R.H. A Soldier's Recollections. Washington, D.C.: Zenger Publishing Company Reprint, 1983.
88. DICK PRICE HANGS ON
Hanifen, Michael. History of Battery B, 1st New Jersey Artillery. Ottowa, Illinois: 1905.
89. VIEW FROM A LITTER
Stiles, Robert. Four Years Under Marse Robert. Neale Publishing Company, 1903.
90. THE HOGS ATE IT UP!
Autobiography of Captain Richard W. Musgrove. Privately published by Mary D. Musgrove, 1921.
91. OFFICERS' DRESS
Worsham, John H. One of Jackson's Foot Cavalry. Ed. B.I. Wiley. Jackson, Tennessee: 1964.
92. ANOTHER LOOK AT HENRY WENTZ
Diary and Memoirs of Rufus W. Jacklin (unpublished), University of Michigan Library.
93. THE DEAD MAN "STOOD UP"
White, Colonel Russ, U.S.M.C. Diary of Sergeant W.S. White. Privately printed.
94. INCIDENT ON THE PLANK FARM
Confederate Veteran, Vol. 8, 1900.
95. THE JAMES RIVER BROTHERS
Memoir of Clarissa F. Jones. Philadelphia North American. June 29, 1913.
96. DEATH BE NOT PROUD
Foster, John Y. "Four Days at Gettysburg." Harper's Magazine, February, 1864.
97. A REBEL "SCAM"
Diary of Isaac Harris, U.S. Sanitary Commission Agent. Pennsylvania State Library.
98. THE DEFIANT COLONEL
Jones, H.G. To the Christian Soldiers and Sailors of the Union. Philadelphia: Lippincott's Press, 1868.
99. THEIR FIFTH SON
A Gettysburg Girl's Story of the Great Battle. Privately published, 1900.
100. THE SHARPSHOOTER'S SKELETON
Campbell, John T. "Letter." National Tribune, September 17, 1908.
101. A "METHODIST NUN"
Deceased Sisters. Notes on Sister Mary David Solomon. 1932.
102. THE DOCTOR FINDS HIS BROTHER
Confederate Veteran, Vol. 22, 1914.

03. THE WANDERING PIG
    Letter of Emory Sweetland, 154th New York, to his parents. Author's collection. July 26, 1863.
04. A "PLUCKY" JOHNNIE
    Wert, J.H. "In the Hospitals of Gettysburg." Harrisburg Telegraph, July 27, 1907.
05. THE WOUNDED WOMAN REBEL
    Letter of Thomas Read, Company E, 5th Michigan, to his parents. University of Michigan Library, August 20, 1863.
06. GLOWING GRAVES
    Johnson, Clifton, ed. Battleground Adventures. Boston: Houghton Mifflin Company, 1915.
    Taylor, William H. "Some Experiences of a Confederate Assistant Surgeon." 19th Virginia, 1906. (Paper read to College of Physicians of Philadelphia.)
07. THE "DUTCH" FARMER
    Bacon, G.W. and E.W. Howland. Letters of a Family During the War for the Union, 1861-1865. Vol. II, 1899.
08. HUMAN SPECIMENS
    Memoir of J.E. Jacobs.
    Report of General Agent of State of New York. Albany, New York: 1864.
09. RISQUE BUSINESS
    Wert, J.H. "In the Hospitals of Gettysburg." Harrisburg Telegraph, July 27, 1907.
10. THE PRESIDENT'S NEPHEW
    Memoir of Clarissa F. Jones. Philadelphia North American. June 29, 1913.
11. ESCAPE FROM LETTERMAN
    Confederate Veteran, November, 1901.
12. THE SLEEPING REB
    Letter to a friend from Frank Stoke. Gettysburg College Library, Gettysburg, Pennsylvania.
13. THE DEADLY PHOTOGRAPH
    Bucklin, Sophronia E. In Hospital and Camp. Philadelphia: 1869.
14. "I DON'T SEE IT, BOYS!"
    Holstein, Anna M. Three Years in the Field Hospital of the Army of the Potomac. Philadelphia: 1867.
15. ONE WOMAN'S DEVOTION
    Cross, Andrew B. Battle of Gettysburg and the Christian Commission. 1865
    Hackett, H.B. Christian Memorials of the War. Boston: 1864.
16. THE PERFECT STUMP
    Ebersole, Jacob, M.D. Incidents of Field Hospital LIfe with the Army of the Potomac. Ohio MOLLUS, Vol. 4.
17. AN HONEST OFFICER
    Army and Navy Journal, September, 1863.
18. CLOSE CALLS
    Research notes in author's files.
19. ADAMS COUNTY CIVILIANS
    Research notes in author's files.

PART VI

20. THESE HONORED DEAD?
    Information from Kathy G. Harrison, Gettysburg National Military Park Library.
21. MISS "TOMMY" KAMOO
    Lancaster Examiner, March 2, 1904.
22. DEADLY EXPLOSIVES AFTER MANY YEARS
    McCreary, A. "A Boy's Experience of the Battle." McClure's, 1909.
23. A GHOST STORY
    "Mrs. Bigham's Story," The Gettysburg Times, April 22, 1941.
24. AN OPERATION PERFORMED 21 YEARS LATER
    Grand Army Scout and Sentinel, Vol. 4, No. 9.
25. A FIFTY-YEAR-OLD "FIND"
    Whitaker, W.P. Confederate Veteran, Vol. 21, November, 1913.
26. LOST AT GETTYSBURG
    Special Dispatch to The North American, October 26, 1899.
27. HE VISITED HIS OWN GRAVE
    Wert, J.H. "In the Hospitals of Gettysburg." Harrisburg Telegraph, No. 10., July-August, 1907.
28. THEY MET AGAIN 50 YEARS LATER
    Literary Digest article, page 75, July, 1913.
29. THE LONG LOST SWORD HILT
    Gilmore, D.M. "With Gregg at Gettysburg."
    Glimpses of the Nation's Struggle. Minnesota (MOLLUS) War Papers, Fourth Series. St. Paul: H.L. Collins Co., 1898.
30. THE STORY OF A BULLET
    The Grand Army Scout and Soldier's Mail, Vol. 4, 1884.

Gregory Ashton Coco was born in 1946, and grew up around Mansura, Avoyelles Parish, Louisiana. He graduated from the University of Southwestern Louisiana in 1972 with a bachelors degree in history. From 1967-1969, Coco served in the U.S. Army, spending 13 months in Vietnam with the 25th Infantry Division as an interrogator and infantryman. Wounded twice in combat, he returned to Louisiana where he worked as a city policeman and state trooper before moving to Gettysburg in 1975. In 1976, Coco became a Licensed Battlefield Guide, and a year later a park ranger with the National Park Service.

For the last several years he has worked as an historian with the National Park Service and the U.S. Army. In 1981, Coco published "Through Blood and Fire: The Civil War Letters of Charles J. Mills," and is currently writing a guide to the Union and Confederate field hospitals which were in operation at Gettysburg from July to November of 1863.

If the reader has any questions concerning the stories in this booklet, please feel free to write the author at Bendersville, Pennsylvania 17306-0400.

John S. Heiser was born and raised in Raleigh, North Carolina, an area rich in history. He has had an interest in the Civil War since the age of six, and continuing this interest, John received his degree in American History from Western Carolina University. An employee for the National Park Service since 1978, he has also contributed illustrations and maps for other works on the subject, including the three volumes of The Vicksburg Campaign, by Edwin Bearss.

My profound thanks go out to good friends Bob Moore, John Heiser, and Kathy Georg Harrison for their assistance in making this booklet possible. But most especially, I appreciate the work and time donated by Cindy L. Small, my compadré and spouse forever.